CRAVE
MINNEAPOLIS
ST. PAUL

The Urban Girl's Manifesto

Melody Biringer

The Urban Girl's Manifesto

We CRAVE Community.
At CRAVE Minneapolis/St. Paul we believe in acknowledging, celebrating, and passionately supporting local businesses. We know that, when encouraged to thrive, neighborhood establishments enhance communities and provide rich experiences not usually encountered in mass-market. We hope that, by introducing you to the savvy business women in this guide, CRAVE Minneapolis/St. Paul will help inspire your own inner entrepreneur.

We CRAVE Adventure.
We could all use a getaway, and at CRAVE Minneapolis/St. Paul we believe that you don't need to be a jet setter to have a little adventure. There's so much to do and to explore right in your own backyard. We encourage you to break your routine, to venture away from your regular haunts, to visit new businesses, to explore all the funky finds and surprising spots that the Twin Cities have to offer. Whether it's to hunt for a birthday gift, indulge in a spa treatment, order a bouquet of flowers, or connect with like-minded people, let CRAVE Minneapolis/St. Paul be your guide for a one-of-a-kind hometown adventure.

We CRAVE Quality.
CRAVE Minneapolis/St. Paul is all about quality products and thoughtful service. We know that a satisfying shopping trip requires more than a simple exchange of money for goods, and that a rejuvenating spa date entails more than a quick clip of the cuticles and a swipe of polish. We know you want to come away feeling uplifted, beautiful, excited, relaxed, relieved and, above all, knowing you got the most bang for your buck. We have scoured the city to find the hidden gems, new hot spots, and old standbys, all with one thing in common: they're the best of the best!

A Guide to our Guide

CRAVE Minneapolis/St. Paul is more than a guidebook. It's a savvy, quality-of-lifestyle book devoted entirely to the best local businesses owned by women. CRAVE Minneapolis/St. Paul will direct you to more than 100 local spots—top boutiques, spas, cafes, stylists, fitness studios, and more. And we'll introduce you to the inspired, dedicated women behind these exceptional enterprises, for whom creativity, quality, innovation, and customer service are paramount. Not only is CRAVE Minneapolis/St. Paul an intelligent guidebook for those wanting to know what's happening throughout town, it's a directory for those who value the contributions that spirited businesswomen make to our city.

Consumer Business Section
Consumer-driven entreprenesses, including boutiques, spas, and food.

Intelligentsia Section
Business-to-business entreprenesses, including coaching, marketing and public relations, photography, business consulting, and design services.

CRAVE Categories
ABODE - Home/interior design related goods and services.
ADORN - Jewelry-related goods and services.
CHILDREN'S - Baby, children, and mom-related goods and services.
CONNECT - Networking, media, technology, and event services.
DETAILS - Miscellaneous goods and services.
ENHANCE - Spa, salon, beauty, fitness studios, and personal trainers.
SIP SAVOR - Food, drink, and caterers.
STYLE - Clothing, shoes, eyewear, handbags, stylists, etc.
PETS - Pet-related goods and services.

What do you CRAVE? In business? In life?

" *Family, friends, clients, and vodka — with olives!* "

Becky Sturm of StormSister Spatique

the 3/50 project

3 What three independently owned businesses would you miss if they disappeared? Stop in. Say hello. Pick up something that brings a smile. Your purchases keep those businesses around.

50 If half the employed population committed $50 of their current monthly spending to locally owned independent businesses, it would generate more than $42.6 billion in revenue. Imagine the positive impact if 3/4 of the employed population did that.

68 For every $100 spent in locally owned independent businesses, $68 returns to the community through taxes, payroll, and other expenditures. If you spend that in a national chain, only $43 stays here. Spend it online and *nothing comes home*.

1 The number of people it takes to start the trend...*you.*

Pick 3. Spend 50. Save your local economy.

LEARN MORE AT
the350project.net

FACEBOOK.COM/THE350PROJECT

Shop Local

Good for you, and good for your community—that's CRAVE's take on shopping local. Small businesses add character and pizzazz to your neighborhood, and by supporting them you're doing your part to enhance local flavor even more. If you're like us and can't imagine life without your favorite locally owned businesses, make an effort to shop locally as often as you can. It's surprising—and awesome!—how huge the impact can be on boosting revenue in your community. Plus, it's a perfect excuse to go shopping!

About the 3/50 Project

Built on the premise "Pick 3, spend 50, save your local economy," The 3/50 Project exploded onto the national stage in March 2009, helping consumers recognize they could have a positive impact on their communities simply by supporting local, independent businesses. Committing just $50 per month to those businesses makes a difference. What three stores would you miss if they disappeared?

Contact

the350project.net, Twitter: @cindabaxter, facebook.com/the350project

Cinda Baxter

Photo by Jessica Barker Photography

Q and A

What are your most popular products or services?
Our core message. We're the first "buy local" program that embraces balance—not the typical all-or-nothing approach.

People may be surprised to know...
The 3/50 Project began with a blog post and no business plan. Who knew it would go viral in five days?

What or who inspired you to start your business?
My frustration with negativity. Why get stuck in the muck when you can say, "Let's fix this thing!" instead?

How do you spend your free time?
Playing with tech gadgets and reading. I'm such a nerd.

For my Mother Love you always.

Q and A

What are your most popular products or services?
A romantic stroll in the vineyards, walking through the cellar door for a wine tasting, without having to leave Minnesota to go somewhere else.

What or who inspired you to start your business?
My father. I'm living out his fantasy.

Who is your role model or mentor?
Joan of Arc. Crazy, but with great conviction.

What business mistake have you made that you will not repeat?
We planted our vineyard in the '70s. Know what land prices were like back then in Napa Valley?

How do you spend your free time?
Drinking other people's wine.

Nan Bailly

ALEXIS BAILLY VINEYARD

18200 Kirby Ave, Hastings, 651.437.1413
abvwines.com, facebook.com/alexisbaillyvineyard

Red. Red. Wine.

Nestled in the lush Hiawatha Valley of the Upper Mississippi is the Alexis Bailly Vineyard. Nan Bailly, master winemaker, has earned Minnesota unlikely fame in the wine-drinking world for her award-winning wines, including "Best Wine In America" for her Voyageur at the prestigious Atlanta International Wine Competition. She embraces her motto enthusiastically: "where the grapes can suffer, but wine drinkers will not!"

ALFRESCO CASUAL LIVING

321 S Main St, Stillwater, 651.439.0814
alfrescocasualliving.com, facebook.com/alfrescocasualliving

Stylish. Trendy. Unique.

Alfresco Casual Living is a retail destination for the entire metro area, featuring the latest in design and trend. From Pine Cone Hill bedding and Company C area rugs, to baby gifts and tabletop items, they have it all. Located in a hundred-year-old warehouse building, Alfresco offers more than 5,000 square feet of gifts, home furnishings, garden accessories, and much more.

Meg Brownson

What are your most popular products or services?
Pine Cone Hill bedding, Company C rugs,
Mariposa, Michael Aram, and Peggy Karr glass.

People may be surprised to know...
How much can be special ordered for their home.

What or who inspired you to start your business?
When I found out the space in this building
would be available, I knew immediately that I
wanted to open a specialty retail store here.

How do you spend your free time?
With my family; boating, cooking,
grilling on the patio, and walking.

Where is your favorite place to
go with your girlfriends?
Downtown to my girlfriend's restaurants!
(Savories Bistro and Dock Cafe!)

What is your indulgence?
Baths!

Amy Zaroff

People may be surprised to know...
I started my career in television production,
went on to own a restaurant with my husband,
and decided to pursue event planning
to combine the best of both worlds.

Who is your role model or mentor?
My grandfather. He always said "at the end
of the day, all you have is your name."

What business mistake have you
made that you will not repeat?
Not being part of a business peer group early
in my career. Now that I am, I have expanded
my potential in more ways than I could ever
imagine. Having smart women from different
backgrounds around you as you navigate your
business allows you to bounce ideas off of
women who have made the same decisions,
choices, and mistakes as you have.

AMY ZAROFF
EVENTS AND DESIGN

7179 Washington Ave S, Edina, 952.941.3371
amyzaroff.com, Twitter: @amyzaroff, facebook.com/amyzaroffeventsanddesign

Authentic. Visionary. Chic.
At Amy Zaroff Events and Design, events are not a hobby, they are a passion.
Creative, innovative, and stylish are just a few ways clients describe their work.
A love of all things party and paper, paired with solid attention to detail, make
this the go-to studio for weddings, mitzvahs, and corporate events alike.

Ann Bancroft Foundation

Reach. Explore. Discover.

Ann Bancroft

Q and A

What are your most popular
products or services?
With a Dare to Dream Micro Grant, a girl
discovers her passion and explores her
dream. The Annual Dream Maker Awards
Event recognizes and honors individuals
and organizations for achievement
and support of women and girls.

People may be surprised to know...
Micro grants are powerful! Giving girls
from diverse backgrounds the opportunity
to explore new experiences can make
a profound difference in their lives. Our
generous donors make this happen.

What or who inspired you to start your business?
I was lucky—my family supported my dreams,
and I became the first woman to reach the
North and South Poles. I realized I could use
my experiences to inspire girls, and help them
navigate their way toward their dreams.

ANN BANCROFT FOUNDATION

808 14th Avenue SE, Minneapolis, 612.676.9484
annbancroftfoundation.org, facebook.com/annbancroftfoundation

Reach. Explore. Discover.

The Ann Bancroft Foundation (ABF) supports girls and women so they can realize their highest dreams and potential. The foundation recognizes individual achievement and promotes initiatives that inspire courage, risk-taking, integrity, and individuality. Thoughtful in its use of resources and the guidance it gives its grant recipients, ABF provides donors the satisfaction of really making a difference in the lives of the next generation.

15

ARAFINA

3365 Galleria, Edina, 952.925.1565
arafina.com, Twitter: @arafina, facebook.com/arafinacontemporaryfashion

Sophisticated. Modern. Feminine.
Arafina is a fashion-forward specialty store that offers upscale contemporary designers, such as Theory, Helmut Lang, Alice and Olivia, Robert Rodriguez, and Nanette Lepore. New designers are added every season. Arafina also specializes in contemporary social occasion clothes—dresses, gowns, and dressy separates—and accessories to complete the looks.

What are your most popular products or services?
Our trend-right but classic vibe, great dresses and "going-out" tops, social dress registry, and rewards for best customers.

What or who inspired you to start your business?
In 1998, there were very few fashion specialty stores in the TC. I wanted to help fill the void.

Who is your role model or mentor?
Barney's, Bergdorf's, and Bendel's.

How do you spend your free time?
Owning a business means not having much free time! But, I do attend the opera, entertain, and travel.

Ann Ackman

Stephanie Haenes

Q and A

What are your most popular
products or services?
Chrome Hearts and Alain Mikli eyewear,
as well as Tag Heuer sunwear is popular.
And everyone loves Dr. Haupert. His
eye exams are extraordinary.

People may be surprised to know...
Some of the most exclusive eyewear
in my store takes a full two months to
manufacture. It sees three countries
before ending up on the shelves!

What or who inspired you to
start your business?
I had so many ideas about how I thought
an optical business should be run, and
nobody was listening. I finally decided to
take my ideas and open my own shop!

ART OF OPTIKS

747 E Lake St, Wayzata, 952.404.2020
artofoptiks.com, facebook.com/artofoptiks

Attentive. Exceptional. Luxurious.
Art of Optiks is an award-winning luxury purveyor of handmade and limited edition eyewear.
Accepting most insurance plans, they provide outstanding eye-care services ranging from eye
exams and complicated contact lens fittings to dry-eye management and eye-disease care.

Photos by Maya K. Photography

19

Photos by Stacy Dunlap

BANANA SHULL INTERIOR DESIGN

275 Market St, Ste 564, Minneapolis, 612.455.2664
bananashull.com, facebook.com/bananashullid

Crisp. Comfortable. Classic.
Banana Shull Interior Design is a complete design studio that provides the luxury
of helping you explore your personal style: color consulting, space planning, and
furniture selections. The design firm offers experience in working with architects and
contractors on new or remodeled construction with an environmental awareness.
BSID is nationally recognized for designing innovative and creative spaces.

Banana Shull

People may be surprised to know...
Using an interior designer is like using
a travel agent. We get you there faster,
and it's lots of fun when you arrive.

Who is your role model or mentor?
My mentors are Larry Mork and Bob
Lennox, the first designers I worked for in
Minneapolis. They were gifted and wildly
fun. My role model is Vincent Wolf, who has
a good sense of humor and irreverent style.
He incorporates his travel escapades into
his design; old and new, ethnic and sleek.

How do you spend your free time?
I love to fly fish... to cast a good line is as
much fun as a great shot in any sport.

What do you CRAVE? In business? In life?
Art! It makes all the difference in adding
soul, color, and pizzazz to a space.

Q and A

Sheila Vaccaro

What are your most popular products or services?
Baby gifts, such as the Euro-style tub, cloth diapers, and organics. Shoppers also value special ordering and free gift wrap.

Who is your role model or mentor?
My 93-year-old mom, who is still open to new ideas and continues to be my treasured sounding board.

What or who inspired you to start your business?
My sister suggested this business to me. It was a perfect fit because I'm a teacher and do-er, and I love children, clothing, and design.

How do you spend your free time?
Reading, decorating, cooking, sewing, and watching games and performances by my teen grandkids.

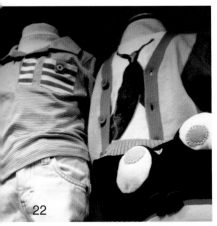

BANANAS FOR KIDS

1157 E Wayzata Blvd, Wayzata, 952.473.3383
bananasforkids.com, facebook.com/bananasforkids

Timeless. Trendy. Treasured.

Dress 'em while you can! Kids and grown-ups agree these are the best clothes and gifts ever for newborns, boys up to 7 or 8 years old, and tween girls. Carefully selected lines are made in the United States, Europe, and by local designers. Casual-to-dressy and trendy-to-timeless styles are presented in easy-to-shop stations in a bright and cheerful atmosphere.

BELLA ON THE BAY SPA SALON

474 2nd St, Excelsior, 952.474.5005
bellaonthebay.com, facebook.com/BellaBay

BELLA SALON AND SPA

3811 W 50th St, Edina, 612.928.7835
bellasalonedina.com

Cozy. Beautiful. Cutting-Edge.

Bella Salon and Spa in the 50th and France area offers a NY Soho feel, a hip location that blends cutting-edge techniques in a high-energy social environment. Bella on the Bay in Excelsior off Lake Minnetonka has a more Hampton feel. The same techniques are blended in a warm, intimate space, with an extensive spa to soothe and rejuvenate your well-being.

Pamela Cruz

What or who inspired you to start your business?
I was inspired by my mother growing up; she had her own salon. Scott Cole was also a great inspiration because I admired his education and love for art. I was inspired to start Bella Salon and Spa after having my twins and wanting to be in control of my own destiny.

Who is your role model or mentor?
Vivianne McKinder was my mentor, she was the first female director of Vidal Sassoon, she mixed cutting-edge technique with feminine beauty, and I'll never forget that.

What do you CRAVE? In business? In life?
I crave to provide excellence in everything I do, from a simple haircut and color, to owning my own business. I want to ensure that I provide not only a service, but also an education to my clients. In life, I want to make sure that every person knows how important they are to me.

BELLAPAMELLA

Twin Cities
bellapamella.com, Twitter: @pamellawith2ls, facebook.com/bellapamella

Fun. Stylish. Smart.
BellaPamella.com, recognized by Rachael Ray and Martha Stewart, is home to positively perfect aprons and the "Never-Ending-List-Of-Very-BellaPamella-Ideas." The Idea blog, infused with Pam Mariutto's personal brand of humor, creativity, and lifestyle, is an invaluable resource toward the fight against disorganization and the general stress of being a mom today. Life's messy. Wearing a fabulous apron helps!

Photos by Erica Loeks Photography

Pam Mariutto

Q and A

What are your most popular products or services?
The matching mom, daughter, and baby
items. Also, the Lucy Hair Snug.

People may be surprised to know...
I'm a career mom who realized if I
couldn't be the perfect domestic goddess,
I could at least look the part!

What or who inspired you to start your business?
I saw an exhibit of vintage aprons
and thought, "I want that!"

What business mistake have you
made that you will not repeat?
Rachael Ray "favorited" us. It created such a
buzz, we sold-out that apron in two weeks! We
could've sold two or three times as many.

Roxy Freese

What are your most popular products or services?
Locally-made items, fair-trade and eco product, jewelry, and whimsical home accessories are just a few of our customers' favorites.

People may be surprised to know...
Bibelot offers a complimentary recyclable box and ribbon with every gift—especially helpful at holiday time!

What or who inspired you to start your business?
Saint Anthony Park in 1966 was simply the right place and the right time to begin the Bibelot adventure.

Who is your role model or mentor?
Beauty was important to my mother. She had amazing taste with an openness to all things creative.

BIBELOT

1082 Grand Ave, St. Paul, 651.222.0321
300 E Hennepin Ave, Minneapolis, 612.379.9300
4315 Upton Ave, Minneapolis, 612.925.3175
2276 Como Ave, St. Paul, 651.646.5651
bibelotshops.com, facebook.com/thebibelotshops

Inspired. Imaginative. Inviting.
Bibelot offers all things delightful—a playful, eclectic collection of goods you never knew you
needed but are thrilled to discover! The shops are brimming with fun and functional gifts, clothing,
jewelry, toys, stationery, and home accents, all artfully displayed. Always fresh and current,
Bibelot has been delighting customers for well over 40 years, leading the way in Twin Cities retail.

Tracy Singleton

Q and A

What are your most popular
products or services?
Families love our local, organic baby food
and kids' meals. Neighbors come for the
friendly service and relaxed atmosphere.
Friends meet over a glass of wine, and
everyone comes for the *good real food*!

People may be surprised to know...
Although we've won many accolades
for "Best Vegetarian Restaurant," our
summertime BLT with Tim Fischer's bacon
and local heirloom tomatoes is tied for top
seller with our wild acres turkey burger.

What or who inspired you to
start your business?
Once I discovered the importance of
knowing where our food comes from
and the joy of connecting with farmers,
I wanted to share it with everyone!

BIRCHWOOD CAFÉ

3311 E 25th St, Minneapolis, 612.722.4474
birchwoodcafe.com, Twitter: @birchwoodcafe, @tweetytracy, facebook.com/BirchwoodCafeMlps

Good. Real. Food.
A crossroads of hot food and cool comfort, Birchwood Café is one part funky coffee house, one part neighborhood cafe, and two parts eclectic organic kitchen. They create fresh, unique food with down-home appeal. Sourcing local, sustainable, organic, and fair-trade ingredients to connect you to the farmers and producers who grow their food, Birchwood Café is more than a restaurant, it's a community!

Photos by Erica Loeks Photography

What is your indulgence?

" *Jelly at breakfast, cookies at lunch, and ice cream before bed.* "

Banana Shull of Banana Shull Interior Design

Danielle Radke

Q and A

What are your most popular
products or services?
Our fabulous bath bombs!

People may be surprised to know...
We make our own products in our secret
little lab in the back of our store!

What or who inspired you to
start your business?
I get the "creative gene" from my mom.
I just went a little crazy with it!

What is your indulgence?
A hot bath (of course!).

Where is your favorite place to
go with your girlfriends?
Any place that we can gab and catch up.

BLISSFUL BATH

9020 Hudson Road, Ste 415, Woodbury, 651.209.9977
blissfulbath.com

Indulgent. Playful. Creative.
Blissful Bath is a fun, unique, and whimsical company that creates delicious
concoctions for bath and body. Their products are designed to resemble cupcakes,
chocolates, pastries, and other delicious indulgences. Why? Because they want
their customers to feel like they have given themselves a decadent treat every time
they use these products. So go ahead, indulge ... a blissful bath awaits you!

Photos by studioTart.

BLOOMA

3919 W 44th St, Edina, 952.848.1111
968 Grand Ave, St. Paul, 952.848.1111
St. Francis Regional Medical Center: 1455 St. Francis Ave, Shakopee, 952.428.3000
blooma.com, Twitter: @bloomayoga, facebook.com/bloomayoga

Joyful. Warm. Meaningful.
Blooma Yoga Studio nurtures the mind-body-heart needs of women and their families. They provide a friendly place for yoga, massage, education, and support for pregnancy and early parenting. Blooma offers prenatal and postnatal yoga, yoga bonding, family yoga, childbirth education, plus classes for active moms looking to get fit, unwind, and connect. They also provide child care during many classes.

Sarah Longacre

People may be surprised to know...
I have no children of my own, but as
of 2009, I have attended more than
425 births—even in Africa!

What or who inspired you to start your business?
Pregnant women—their strength,
and their beautiful bellies!

Who is your role model or mentor?
My doula sisters and the amazing work they
do to support birthing mamas. I couldn't do this
work without them. I am also pretty crazy about
Gurmukh, an amazing yoga instructor in LA.

What business mistake have you
made that you will not repeat?
Overextending myself. Whether you're starting
a family or a business, you must take good,
good care of yourself so you have the heart
and the strength to weather the challenges
while celebrating the sweet times.

BREAD ART

110 3rd St N, Bayport, 651.351.1475
breadart.biz, facebook.com/BreadArt

Scrumptious. Tempting. Fresh.
Bread Art is a family-owned and operated bakery. They bake all of their
outrageously delicious products from scratch in their store. Bread Art offers a
variety of tantalizing handmade breads, pastries, cakes, pies, and other baked
goods. They use only natural ingredients and do not add preservatives or additives.
They bake their fabulous products fresh daily. Come taste the difference!

Photos by Sky Blue Rose Photography

Heather Peterson

Q and A

What are your most popular products or services?
We are best known for our amazing
artisan breads and incredible pastries.

People may be surprised to know...
We have a full line of spectacular
desserts, and we do wedding cakes!

What business mistake have you
made that you will not repeat?
Not asking enough questions and just assuming
that the other person has my best interest at heart.

How do you spend your free time?
With my family, especially watching
my boy's sporting events.

Where is your favorite place to
go with your girlfriends?
We love to go to The Good Earth
and just sit and talk.

Cindy Sudheimer

Q and A

What are your most popular products or services?
Amazing swimwear, cover-ups, and fashionable apparel for women and men.

What or who inspired you to start your business?
I wanted to have a store that reminds you of your favorite vacation boutiques and beach bungalows. A place you really don't want to leave.

Who is your role model or mentor?
Craig DeLongy from "John Craig."

What do you CRAVE? In business? In life?
To be passionate in every aspect of my life.

THE BUNGALOW

229 Water St, Excelsior, 952.474.4537
5619 Manitou Road, Tonka Bay
bungalowbeachwear.com

Inviting. Inspiring. Exotic.
The Bungalow is the kind of store that you want to visit everyday. It has such a comfortable feel—like when you are on vacation and just found the greatest store ever! You will find not only amazing swimwear and cover-ups, but also great tops, jeans, etc, for both women and men.

Photos by Maya K Photography

Linda Haug

Q and A

What are your most popular products or services?
I believe our customers enjoy our take on food: quality ingredients served in a professional, yet unpretentious manner.

People may be surprised to know...
That I enjoy listening to metal.

What or who inspired you to start your business?
My mother's death from cancer 10 years ago brought it home that you only get *this* life.

Who is your role model or mentor?
Julia Child was an early influence. Lucia Watson, for local food sense. My father was my mentor.

How do you spend your free time?
Cooking, riding bikes with my husband late at night, and playing with our cats.

CAFÉ TWENTY EIGHT

2724 W 43rd St, Minneapolis, 612.926.2800
cafetwentyeight.com, Twitter: @CafeTwentyEight

Local. Welcoming. Casual.
Café Twenty Eight has been Linden Hills' neighborhood bistro for more than eight years. They source many of their products from sustainable local farms and suppliers, including Surly Brewing Company, Coffee and Tea LTD., Clancey's, and many others. Owner Linda Haug loves the Linden Hills neighborhood—it has been her home for 17 years, and she couldn't imagine living—or having her business—anywhere else.

Sheela Namakkal and Emily Harris

Q and A

What are your most popular
products or services?
Our cupcakes, especially for weddings!

People may be surprised to know...
We offer many vegan and gluten-
free items, for all dietary needs.

Who is your role model or mentor?
Erik and Gretchen Funk of the Triple
Rock Social Club. Without them,
we'd be lost. Thanks, guys!

What is your indulgence?
Eating and drinking well. Sleeping in.

Where is your favorite place to
go with your girlfriends?
We love the Modern Cafe, Obento-ya, Psycho
Suzi's, and the Red Stag Supperclub.

CAKE EATER BAKERY

2929 E 25th St, Minneapolis, 612.354.7178
cakeeaterbakery.com, Twitter: @cakeeaterbakery, facebook.com/cakeeaterbakery

Innovative. Fun. Delicious.
Cake Eater Bakery is a full-service bakery and coffee shop in the Seward
neighborhood. They specialize in creative and flavorful baked goods and
beverages. Using fresh, local ingredients, they make more than 100 types of
cupcakes and other bakery classics with a modern twist. Cake Eater is available
to cater your next event, including weddings, parties, and office functions.

Photos by studioTart.

CAMROSE HILL FLOWERS

233 S 2nd St, Stillwater, 651.351.9631
camrosehillflowers.com, Twitter: @camrosehill

Natural. Beautiful. Romantic.
Enter the garden gate to this quaint "off the beaten path" shop in downtown Stillwater to find beautiful, natural flower arrangements and nature-inspired gifts for home and garden. Owner Cindie Sinclair also hosts weddings on her beautiful 1880s farm located in rural Stillwater. Check out the Camrose Hill website to see some of the magic of this beautiful, rustic, romantic farm.

Cindie Sinclair

Q and A

What or who inspired you to start your business?
I always wanted to live the Country life. A trip to England cemented that idea for me. I held a vision of an authentic life close to nature, a place I could grow flowers and create my own style. Camrose Hill Farm and the Camrose Hill Retail Shop in Stillwater are the creative expression of that dream. My vision has grown creatively in ways I never would have imagined.

What business mistake have you made that you will not repeat?
In the early years I allowed the stress to overwhelm me—coming up with new creative ideas, keeping the gardens beautiful, running a business, etc. Now I remind myself how wonderful it is to be of service—in helping brides create their vision for their day. I always say, I work with happy people who are in love, and I am so lucky to have work where my contribution is to create beauty and make people happy!

LOVE

CASA VERDE DESIGN

911 W 50th St, Minneapolis, 612.353.4401
casaverdedesign.com, facebook.com/casaverdedesign

Stylish. Classic. Sophisticated.
Casa Verde Design is an award-winning design showroom that specializes in creating custom kitchens and baths that are a unique reflection of each client. These kitchen designs are focused on attention to detail, functionality, and quality materials in a wide range of styles. They offer cabinetry for the entire home, including bathrooms, home offices, media centers, and built-ins.

Photos by Jessica Barker Photography

Rosemary Merrill, Susan Brunn, and Susan Jacobs

 Q and A

What are your most popular products or services?
Kitchen and bath design service with custom cabinetry. Unique home furnishings.

People may be surprised to know...
That it is important to hire a kitchen and bath designer that is skilled at assessing consumer's individual needs by creating designs that meet and exceed these requirements.

What business mistake have you made that you will not repeat?
Don't just believe the sales pitch—take your time and do your own homework to find out for yourself what the best solution should be,

What do you CRAVE? In business? In life?
Honesty, integrity, the ability to keep it in perspective, and a sense of humor!

COCOA & FIG

651 Nicollet Mall, Skyway Level, Saks Wing, Minneapolis, 612.333.1485
cocoaandfig.com, Twitter: @cocoaandfig

Elegent. Fresh. Fun.
At Cocoa & Fig, it's all about the food. Food that is approachable, delicious, comforting, and beautiful. Inspired to create products that make people happy, their secret is: Use only the best ingredients, and make everything from scratch. It may seem surprisingly simple, but it transforms the ordinary to extraordinary. Really, the food speaks for itself, and who doesn't love that!

Laurie Pyle

People may be surprised to know...
We started as a catering company and grew the business based on customer demand. Our pastries get all the attention, but we make fabulous food, too!

Who is your role model or mentor?
I worked for an amazing chef named Sara Foster when I was in culinary school. She taught me the importance of using high-quality ingredients and letting the food speak for itself.

What business mistake have you made that you will not repeat?
Not asking for help when I really, truly needed it.

What is your indulgence?
Southern banana pudding.

Where is your favorite place to go with your girlfriends?
The spa for pedicures.

Q and A

What are your most popular products or services?
Unique variety, and great prices. Our ladies love that we keep our brands fresh and our boutique fashionably inspiring season to season.

People may be surprised to know...
I love to fish! I bait my own hook. My dad taught me everything I know, only to be outfished by a girl. Sorry, Dad!

What or who inspired you to start your business?
Jennifer Catto, whom I once worked for, now a great friend. Jenn was convinced I could do anything, and she helped me believe it.

How do you spend your free time?
I love to exercise, garden, paint, and craft as often as possible. Being with the people I love keeps me smiling.

Angela Hudson

COLLABORATIONS BOUTIQUE

129 1/2 S Main St, Stillwater, 651.430.9100

Savvy. Delightful. Trendy.
Collaborations Boutique is a shop for women of all ages. Collaborations specializes in a large collection of clothing and accessories that help you look and feel your best. They offer great prices on unique clothing, bags, shoes, jewelry, jeans, vintage treasures, locally-made fashions, and more. They hope to tickle your fancy and put a fashionable spring in your step!

Marie Dwyer

Q and A

What are your most popular
products or services?
Cooking classes, culinary events,
and interesting culinary tools.

People may be surprised to know...
That we test, taste, or sample everything
we offer in our stores. Everything.

Who is your role model or mentor?
Martha Kaemmer. Her passion for sharing the
culinary experience has a hand in all our work.

What business mistake have you
made that you will not repeat?
Opening a store in a regional mall.

What do you CRAVE? In business? In life?
A consistent sense of well-being
and a manicure that won't chip.

Photos by Eliesa Johnson of Photogen Inc.

COOKS OF CROCUS HILL

877 Grand Ave, St. Paul, 651.228.1333
3925 W 50th St, Edina, 952.285.1903
cooksofcrocushill.com, Twitter: @cookscrocushill, facebook.com/cooksofcrocushill

Authentic. Experiential. Vibrant.
Cooks of Crocus Hill is a locally owned, independent culinary educator and retailer with two cooking schools and two retail stores selling culinary equipment, kitchen tools, books, and packaged food. Cooks of Crocus Hill holds a belief that life happens in the kitchen, and their environments are grounded in creating and sharing authentic culinary experiences.

Judy Malmon

What are your most popular products or services?
One of our most popular items at Cooqi is our awesome brownies—they are decadent, fudgy, crazy yummy, and probably the most fun of all, no one ever can tell they're gluten-free unless you tell them. Our pizza crust rocks, too.

People may be surprised to know...
I am not that good of a baker, and I am terrible at following a recipe. I think this is why I am a great baking coach—I totally understand all the ways it can go wrong, because I've been there!

What or who inspired you to start your business?
My gluten-intolerant daughter was my inspiration. She was in kindergarten, and had to eat broccoli from her lunch while the other kids ate cupcakes (made from wheat). This broke my heart and compelled me to throw my fist in the air and shout, "Never again!"

COOQI GLUTEN-FREE DELIGHTS

2186 Marshall Ave, St. Paul, 651.645.4433
cooqiglutenfree.com

Delicious. Healthy. Joyful.

Cooqi is the gluten-free bakery of your wildest, most scrumptious dreams. They take the challenge seriously to provide you with uncompromisingly delicious treats that are also good for you. All goodies are made with organic whole-grain flours and natural ingredients in their dedicated gluten-free bakery. Cooqi creates indulgence for your spirit that doesn't hurt your body!

Photos by Sky Blue Rose Photography

COVERED

1201 Lagoon Ave, Minneapolis, 612.825.1610
shopcovered.com, Twitter: @coveredgirls, facebook.com/covered.uptown

Relaxed. Inspiring. Fun.
Covered is *the* spot where stylistas flock for their latest fashion fix. Although premium denim is their specialty, they have a well-edited selection of tops, dresses, shoes, and accessories from your favorite designers. Covered also has their own private label line that is on trend and priced right.

Stacy Larson

What are your most popular products or services?
Denim! We have a reputation as "The girls that can fit anyone." We pride ourselves in helping you find the best pair for you!

What or who inspired you to start your business?
The customers I served in the first store where I worked. I knew they needed a better place to shop in the Twin Cities, and the only way I could create that place was on my own terms, in my own space.

What business mistake have you made that you will not repeat?
Spreading myself too thin. When I opened my second store, the first one suffered so much I had to close it. I don't consider it a failure—it was a launchpad for my bigger, better uptown store!

What do you CRAVE? In business? In life?
Contentment. Knowing that I am doing the best I can and that is good enough! That and the *perfect* pair of jeans!

What do you CRAVE? In business? In life?

"*My purpose in life is to be the blueprint—a leader photographer to help shape a new standard for our world. I will be a legend.*"

Eliesa Johnson of Photogen Inc.

DARN KNIT ANYWAY

Brick Alley Building, 423 S Main St, Stillwater, 651.342.1386
darnknitanyway.com, Twitter: @darnknitanyway, facebook.com/darnknitanyway

Creative. Welcoming. Inspiring.
Darn Knit Anyway is a local source for unique yarns and textiles, handmade gifts, and craft accessories. They are proud to be a place dedicated to providing a creative outlet for novice crafters and local artists alike. Stock up on supplies, browse for gifts, try a class project, or just hang out in the lounge to work on a project and chat with friends.

Photos by LD Photography

Aimee Doyle Pelletier

Q and A

What are your most popular products or services?
Our most popular service is our Knit
101 class. Our beginning knit class runs
two times a week, every week!

People may be surprised to know...
We aren't just a yarn shop. We have a boutique
that showcases accessories and gifts handmade
by Minnesota and Wisconsin artists.

Who is your role model or mentor?
Darn Knit Anyway is a tribute to my
grandmother, Nanny Jean. She taught me
to knit and continues to inspire me.

What do you CRAVE? In business? In life?
I crave a balanced life, a successful
business that people love to come to,
and a happy family. So far, so good!

Stephanie
Patineau

Q and A

What are your most popular
products or services?
Vibrant hand-printed tees from St. Louis,
brilliant handmade jewelry from artists
in New York and Colorado, terra cotta
tiles hand-painted in Maryland.

People may be surprised to know...
I strive to be atypical in my buying...
searching for the undiscovered every time.

Who is your role model or mentor?
My mom. She's my biggest supporter
and a financial wizard. Plus, she's
the best unpaid help in town.

What business mistake have you
made that you will not repeat?
Thinking "fashion" is big-name brands with
big price tags. Not so. Women are looking to
express their individuality, not their sameness.

DICHOTOMY

611 E Lake St, Wayzata, 952.476.0668
shopdichotomy.com

Easy-going. Edited. Evolving.
Comfort is key at this sunny Wayzata lakefront boutique, featuring a well-edited collection of women's clothing, jewelry, accessories, and gifts. From printed dresses and Italian leather belts to luxe cashmere sweaters and super-soft cotton tees, dichotomy offers an abundance of one-of-a-kind choices. Dichotomy is a go-to spot for women who want fabulous service and an ever-expanding fashion perspective.

Photos by Maya K. Photography

DITTO & CO.

Twin Cities, 612.619.5820
dittoandco.com, Twitter: @dittoandco, facebook.com/dittoandco

Quality. Taste. Style.
Gretchen Ditto helps each client project a stylish impression of confidence and competency. She works with her clients to transform their style through custom packages that include custom color analysis, fit and style analysis, closet/wardrobe organization, personal shopping, and signature style creation. Need a speaker for your next event? Gretchen loves to speak on the topics of image and etiquette and she offers Girls Night Out.

Q and A

What are your most popular products or services?
Our Total Transformation package, which includes a custom color analysis, fit and style, closet/wardrobe audit, and shopping.

People may be surprised to know...
We focus on styles that work best for each unique client, not fashion trends that come and go.

What or who inspired you to start your business?
I hired an image consultant a few years ago, and it changed my life.

How do you spend your free time?
Traveling with my husband, playing with my Jack Russell terrier, and enjoying a great glass of wine with friends.

What is your indulgence?
I *love* chandeliers.

Gretchen Ditto

67

People may be surprised to know...
That yes, people really do drop their dogs off for day care, very much like taking a child to day care. The result is a tired and happy dog!

What or who inspired you to start your business?
My dog, Bailey, initially started me thinking about a dog day-care business. She attended a day care in Michigan and loved it!

What business mistake have you made that you will not repeat?
When I first opened my business, I thought I could handle the accounting and tax returns without the help of an accountant. I quickly discovered to let the professionals do what they do best, and hired an accountant to straighten out my mess.

What do you CRAVE? In business? In life?
Happiness and a feeling of purpose.

Wendy Harter

DOG DAYS

2120 Myrtle Ave, St. Paul, 651.642.9663
1752 Grand Ave, St. Paul, 651.699.3905
dogdaysinc.com

Fun. Safe. Friendly.
Dog Days is a welcome alternative to lonely days at home for your pooch, offering a friendly, safe, and fun-filled environment. Whether you need care for your dog just for the day or overnight, no one is more committed to your pet's happiness than Dog Days. Does Fido need a bath or new haircut? They offer grooming services as well.

 Q and A

What are your most popular
products or services?
European antiques, reproduction furniture and
accessories, and interior-design services.

How do you spend your free time?
Cooking, wine tasting, reading, and
walking. Spending time with my husband
and kids traveling, exploring, and creating
memories is a key to my life balance.

What is your indulgence?
Shoes, coats, jewelry, and
purses—I love them all!

Who is your role model or mentor?
My husband, who always supports me and
helps me to be grounded in this business.
Also, the many women in my life that inspire
me and bring out my creative side.

Lori Anderson

EURONEST

5700 W 36th St, Minneapolis, 952.929.2927
euro-nest.com, Twitter: @euronest, facebook.com/euronest

Warm. Inviting. One-of-a-kind.
EuroNest is the Twin Cities' premier home furnishings boutique retailer. According to
European culture, a nest is a place that affords individual or unique refuge or lodging;
a home that is comfortable and rejuvenating to the resident. Bringing one-of-a-kind
European antiques, reproduction furnishings, and accessories to market unlike any other
retailer in the Twin Cities, EuroNest is where you can find unique things for any "nest."

Photos by Sky Blue Rose Photography

What are your most popular products or services?
Balayage hair color and cuts, eyebrow shaping, bikini waxing, and skin care.

What or who inspired you to start your business?
The idea of having an establishment where all service providers work from a place of passion with a continued desire for growth.

How do you spend your free time?
When I can, I love to roller blade, read, and take baths.

What is your indulgence?
A long shower with a full-body exfoliation. Giving myself a mask and eye treatment. Top it off with body oils.

Where is your favorite place to go with your girlfriends?
Anywhere outside on a beautiful summer day.

Leah Simon-Clarke

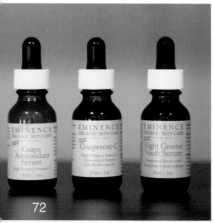

EXTRADOS

4279 Sheridan Ave, Minneapolis, 612.920.0051
3100 W 50th St, Minneapolis, 612.920.0227
824 E Lake St, Wayzata, 952.473.0423
extrados.com, Twitter: @LeahSimonClarke

Classic. Innovative. Dedicated.
Extrados is a specialized, unique salon and spa dedicated to providing only the highest quality service. Their commitment to excellence has received regular attention from local publications, as well as from *The New York Times*, *Cosmopolitan*, *American Salon*, and *Day Spa Magazine*. When you visit Extrados, you will leave feeling like the best version of yourself. When we feel beautiful, we act beautifully.

Photos by Stacy Dunlap

FARAHBEAN

Twin Cities
farahbean.com

Sophisticated. Uncompromising. Confident.
Regarded nationally as true heirloom pieces, farahbean designs are in stores across the country from Japan to the The Museum of Arts and Design in NYC. Each farahbean piece is designed and created by hand by Stephanie and Kristi. From vintage clasps to hand-selected findings, each individual stone is chosen to reflect the unique and incomparable quality of the jewelry.

Q and A

What are your most popular products or services?
People collect our bracelets,
earrings, and necklaces.

People may be surprised to know...
Farahbean was coined from the
designers' childhood nicknames.

What business mistake have you
made that you will not repeat?
Hiring a PR firm in NYC too
early on in our business.

What is your indulgence?
Yoga and great handbags; out
for wine in the evening.

What do you CRAVE? In business? In life?
In business, success to a level where we're
able to share a significant portion with
others. In life, serenity and happiness.

Kristi Anderson and Stephanie Nelson

FARMER'S HAT
PRODUCTIONS

Twin Cities
burburandfriends.com, Twitter: @burbursfriends, facebook.com/burburandfriends

Empowering. Explorative. Educational.
Farmer's Hat Productions, founded by two moms, was created to educate and inspire children ages 2-6 to get active. The Bur Bur & Friends brand is a diverse cast of characters who promote self esteem in kids by teaching them about sports, outdoor exploration, and active play. The characters are based on real children, real moments, and first-time experiences.

JoAnne Pastel and Kakie Fitzsimmons

Q and A

People may be surprised to know...
Our characters are based on actual
children, including our own, and the stories
reflect real first-time experiences.

What or who inspired you to start your business?
We had a hard time finding books and toys
that reflected the reality of our diverse world.
Identifying this unmet niche in the market, we
decided to create our own line of products.

Who is your role model or mentor?
Julie Clark, the founder of Baby Einstein.
We were amazed at how she started,
grew, and sold her business concept.

What do you CRAVE? In business? In life?
That our brand and products inspire many
children and their families to become active
together and make a difference in their lives.

Lindi Dillon

What are your most popular
products or services?
Premium gift baskets with a stylish
flair, personalized stationery, unique
invitations, monogrammed gifts,
and delicious gourmet foods

People may be surprised to know...
I taught 4th grade for many years; I began
to realize that personalization and customer
satisfaction is the key to success—in
the classroom and in business.

Who is your role model or mentor?
My hard-working, dedicated employees
who really make it all happen!

What is your indulgence?
A glass of white burgundy with a grilled
filet mignon and sautéed mushrooms.

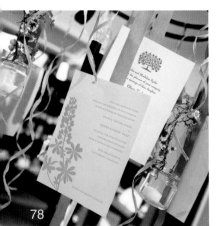

FLEURISH

240 Minnetonka Ave S, Wayzata, 952.476.2296
fleurishllp.com

Frolic. Fresh. Fancy.
Fleurish offers exceptional gifts for all of life's events. Every product has been carefully selected for the customers' shopping experience. They create everything, from custom-designed gift baskets and monogrammed presents, to a perfect wedding shower, baby, or girlfriend gift. Gifts are enhanced by Fleurish's personal touch and unparalleled customer service.

FLIRT BOUTIQUE

177 N Snelling Ave, St. Paul, 651.698.3692
flirt-boutique.com, facebook.com/flirtboutiquemn

Sexy. Sweet. Glamorous.
Flirt is a sexy-sweet lingerie boutique inspired by Hollywood glamour and pin-up girls. Voted best lingerie by *Minnesota Monthly* in 2008 and *City Pages* in 2009, it's clear that Flirt aims to please customers! Flirt carries bras ranging from 32AA-38DDD, filling the niche for quality lingerie in the Twin Cities. Romantic décor and comfortable atmosphere add to the shopping experience.

Photos by Maya K. Photography

Jessica Gerard

Q and A

What are your most popular products or services?
Handpicked bra and panty sets, luxurious
nighties, European hosiery, and a
naughty shelf of bachelorette gifts!

People may be surprised to know...
You can host your party at Flirt. Get exactly what
you want for your shower, or treat your guests.

Who is your role model or mentor?
Pin-up girls, all of them!

What is your indulgence?
Dessert and having the windows down
while the air conditioning is on!

Where is your favorite place to
go with your girlfriends?
I love meeting friends at Nina's Coffee Café.

 Q and A

Andrea Rovner

What are your most popular products or services?
Jewelry, both trend- and designer-inspired! Our selection changes often, as do fashion trends.

People may be surprised to know...
My daughter has been helping me on buying trips for years. She is the true fashionista in our family.

What or who inspired you to start your business?
I wanted to be a role model for my children. Starting my own business in my 40s showed them it's never too late to make things happen in your life.

What is your indulgence?
Designer handbags. I'm a fashion victim.

FRINGE

3906 W 50th St, Edina, 952.746.4922
fringeaccessories.com

Trendy. Chic. Affordable.
Fringe offers the latest trends in women's accessories. Everything from jewelry and handbags to scarves and belts can be found at guilt-free prices. Fringe is a true fashionista's paradise!

Photos by Erica Loeks Photography

83

FUSION LIFESPA

18142 Minnetonka Blvd, Deephaven, 952.345.3335
fusionlifespa.com

Beauty. Balance. Bliss.
Fusion LifeSpa seeks health, beauty, and rejuvenation in one inspired dwelling. Part organic spa, part natural health clinic, they offer the finest in holistic beauty services and time-honored health treatments from highly trained, unique practitioners. The exclusive Fusion Skin Care line represents the highest level of pure, results-oriented skin care by combining the finest botanical ingredients with the latest technology.

Donna Duffy

What are your most popular products or services?
Our organic anti-aging, skin rejuvenation
facials and, for home care, our goat
cheese and fruit purée peels.

People may be surprised to know...
I had horrible acne as a teenager. That is
what inspired me to become an esthetician.

What or who inspired you to start your business?
My mom. I was 23 and complaining about my
boss, and my mom asked me how I would do
things differently. Two weeks later, she emptied
ALL her savings and sent me a check for
$9,999 to start my own business with a card
that said "May all your dreams come true."

Where is your favorite place to
go with your girlfriends?
Fuji Ya for sushi. I *love* sushi!

GALLERI M.

4404 Abbott Ave S, Minneapolis, 612.920.3600

Creative. Colorful. Community.
Galleri M. is an evolving space that wholly supports art in the Twin Cities.

Photos by Sky Blue Rose Photography

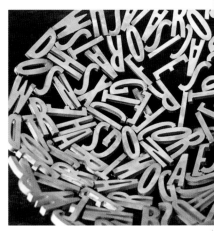

Michelle Dudar

Q and A

What are your most popular products or services?
Art, in every medium.

People may be surprised to know...
Galleri M. supports the environment so much
that we give discounts on art for people
that walk, bike, or bus to our location.

What business mistake have you
made that you will not repeat?
When in doubt go east, not west.

How do you spend your free time?
Bikram yoga, and hanging out with
my lovely, inspirational children.

What is your indulgence?
I can never get enough yoga or raw foods!

What business mistake have you made that you will not repeat?

" *Mistakes? There is no such thing as a mistake. There is learning, and my life has been full of that.* "

Kate-Madonna Hindes of girl.meets.geek

Linda Kleinbaum

Q and A

What are your most popular
products or services?
Our Private Label line enables customers
to explore and craft their own personal
scent, providing a liberating way to
communicate their uniqueness to the world.

People may be surprised to know...
Since 1972, we've been refilling bottles, selling
cruelty-free products, and focusing on the
environment. I am the second generation
in the family to further these ideals.

Where is your favorite place to
go with your girlfriends?
Spending time with friends at
home is best for me. I love relaxing
conversations and sharing ideas.

What do you CRAVE? In business? In life?
Sustainability for the earth, and
compassion for its people.

GARDEN OF EDEN INC.

867 Grand Ave, St. Paul, 651.293.1300
gardenofedenstores.com

Creative. Unique. Empowering.
Garden of Eden specializes in natural bath and body products, home fragrance, and unique items from around the globe. The Private Label line is perfect for adding a custom fragrance to quality bath gels, lotions, hair care, and body sprays. For those who are sensitive, unscented is also an option. Choose from perfume and essential oils to create your own scent.

GFN PRODUCTIONS
GROWING FAMILIES NATURALLY

Twin Cities, 507.304.1810
gfnproductions.com

Authentic. Inspiring. Educational.
Growing Families Naturally events are national zero-waste expos with
inspiring and enlightening speakers, educational panels, hands-on activities
for the whole family, and boutique shopping. With GFN Productions, you
will find a valuable and meaningful experience within each event.

 $\mathcal{Q}$ and $\mathcal{A}$

Holly Jones and Nichole Hirsch Kuechle

What or who inspired you to start your business?
GFN Productions was grown from a desire to educate families nationwide on the benefits of healthy living via a solid platform of experience, and to promote other mompreneurs.

What business mistake have you made that you will not repeat?
Not following our gut, and not checking in with each other.

How do you spend your free time?
At the cabin with family: hiking, boating, playing, and reading.

Where is your favorite place to go with your girlfriends?
A brainstorm retreat.

What do you CRAVE? In business? In life?
Being challenged, pushing the envelope, trying new things, leaps of faith, and bringing what we do full-circle and back home to benefit our families.

Heather Thomas

Q and A

What or who inspired you to
start your business?
Dani Levi, founder of Daily Candy, and
Jen Lancaster, author of *Bitter is the New
Black*—both are business savvy and witty.

Who is your role model or mentor?
Coco Chanel, because she did it *all*
with style. "A girl should be two things:
classy and fabulous."—Coco Chanel.

What business mistake have you
made that you will not repeat?
Always stay true to your brand. Trust your gut.
A woman's intuition is strong and usually right.

What is your indulgence?
Costume jewelry, chocolate, and
anything with a four-inch heel.

GIGISGUIDE.COM

Twin Cities, 612.590.8913
gigisguide.com, Twitter: @gigisguide, facebook.com/gigisguide

Smart. Stylish. Connected.
Gigi's guide is the source for what's hot in the Twin Cities and beyond. Gigi's guide handpicks the latest "musts" in products, businesses, and services for the girl on the go. They research it, experience it, and let you know if it's worth your time. Weekly e-Scoops deliver quick insider tips, along with exclusive discounts and giveaways.

Photos by Erica Loeks Photography

Photos by studioTart.

GOLDEN FIG
FINE FOODS

790 Grand Ave, St. Paul, 651.602.0144
goldenfig.com, Twitter: @goldenfig, facebook.com/goldenfigfinefoods

Sustainable. Delicious. Fantastic.
Golden Fig is a gem of a shop located on historic Grand Avenue. All items stocking the shelves are straight from the Midwest family farm or other small producer. Featuring artisan chocolates, small batch spice blends, hand-crafted cheeses, and many more all-local goodies to tempt your palate, make your dinners fantastic, and make every gift you give be beyond exceptional!

Q and A

Laurie L. Crowell

What are your most popular products or services?
Sel de Cuisine is our savory, tasty seasoning that's fantastic on everything. The butter almond toffee is outrageously delicious!

What business mistake have you made that you will not repeat?
Trying to do everything myself! There are things I am good at, and that is where I strive to spend my time.

How do you spend your free time?
There isn't much free time, but if there is, it involves an adventure of some sort with my husband and our sweet little boys.

What or who inspired you to start your business?
All the farmers and producers I kept meeting that had nowhere to sell their fantastic wares on a regular basis.

What is your indulgence?
Foot reflexology followed by a pedicure.

GUILD

4414 Excelsior Blvd, St. Louis Park, 952.378.1815
guildcollective.wordpress.com

Inspiring. Swanky. Sure thing.
The partners in Guild combine their talents and expertise to create the ultimate boutique experience. Their 3,000 square foot space is visually stunning and packed to the rafters with vintage and new merchandise designed to inspire the most discriminating shoppers. Guild successfully covers every price range ... from hostess gifts to "where in the world did you find *that*?" pieces. It won't disappoint!

Photos by Maya K. Photography

Shayne Barseness, Kelly Dorsey, Jennifer Finlay, Ann Garrity, Nancy Koch, Gwen Leeds, Sheila Leiter, Laurie Luehmann, Donna Menne, Pam Mondale, Debra Pesek, Tami Roth, Sandy Stewart, Daune Stinson, Laura Soetebier, and Lynn Soetebier

Q and A

What are your most popular products or services?
Our "Second Saturday" events are extremely popular. Each month we offer a themed event, including trunk shows, new line launches, styling seminars, makeovers, etc. They're fun and entertaining, we love doing them, and our customers leave having had a great experience.

People may be surprised to know...
Our original plan was to be a temporary "pop-up" store, open only for the 2009 holiday season.

How do you spend your free time?
When not with our families, we all spend our free time scouring for and creating treasures to bring to Guild. That is a passion for all of us, so it may sound like work, but it doesn't feel like work.

Jillian Moriarty

Q and A

People may be surprised to know...
GuruCrew is the sole provider for all
yoga, Pilates, and cardio fitness classes
for Target corporate headquarters.

What or who inspired you to
start your business?
As a physical therapist, I recognized a
huge need for both preventative wellness
and post-rehabilitative care through
individualized, quality instruction.

Who is your role model or mentor?
I am inspired by all my patients who
are so motivated and determined to
improve their health and enjoy life!

What do you CRAVE? In business? In life?
Helping people feel better within themselves
and remembering what is truly important
in life: family, friends, health, and love!

gurucrew

GURUCREW

2519 Cross Point Road, Minnetonka Beach, 612.860.1113
gurucrewmn.com

Therapeutic. Holistic. Dynamic.
GuruCrew is a network of highly qualified yoga, Pilates, and fitness instructors; physical therapists; and Thai bodywork and shiatsu practitioners, available for in-home and corporate hire throughout the Twin Cities. GuruCrew excels at hands-on, personalized care to help clients achieve improved mind-body wellness. The "Tree Fort" studio, located in Minnetonka Beach, offers ongoing classes and Pilates equipment.

Jillian Moriarty

Q and A

What or who inspired you to
start your business?
Becoming a mom inspired me to combine my
physical therapy, yoga, and Pilates expertise
with my love for kids and belief in family first!

What business mistake have you
made that you will not repeat?
Not listening to my inner self and
following my gut instinct.

How do you spend your free time?
Getting outside whenever I can to ski,
skate, boat, swim, garden, play, barbeque,
and socialize with family and friends!

What do you CRAVE? In business? In life?
Health, fun, and a balance between family time
and my career. Happily Ever Active inspires
other families to achieve this balance too!

HAPPILY EVER ACTIVE

Twin Cities, 888-9-HAPPILY (4277459)
livehappilyeveractive.com, Twitter: @happilyeveract, facebook.com/happilyeveractive

Interactive. Healthy. Fun.
Happily Ever Active (HEA) brings families and friends of all ages together to bond and become healthier and happier through fitness and wellness programs. Developed by allied health professionals, classes such as Fit2gether®, Cook2gether®, and Storyoga® blend yoga, Pilates, nutrition, literacy and language, and alternative health therapies. HEA offers a line of high-quality DVDs, gear to wear, and nationwide teacher certification courses.

HUNT & GATHER

4944 Xerxes Ave S, Minneapolis, 612.455.0250
huntandgatherantiques.com

Fresh. Funky. Fashion-forward.
Hunt & gather is a stylish, edited antique shop. This jam-packed, two-level, 20-dealer shop only carries the good stuff. From rustic to retro, discover great finds, including furniture, advertising, oil paintings, taxidermy, architectural elements, textiles, flashcards, letters, and always the unexpected.

Q and A

What or who inspired you to start your business?
The "thrill of the hunt" inspires me daily.

Who is your role model or mentor?
Anyone who gets out there and
digs up the *good* goods!

How do you spend your free time?
Digging around flea markets and
estate sales. I can't get enough!

What is your indulgence?
A grand meal followed by a nightly bath
with a magazine or design book.

**Where is your favorite place to
go with your girlfriends?**
Many of my good friends are in the shop.
We always go to sales/flea markets
together, followed by a great meal and a
"show and tell" of what we all found.

Kristi Berkvam Stratton

I LIKE YOU

501 1st Ave NE, Minneapolis, 612.208.0249
ilikeyouonline.com, Twitter: @ilikeyoumpls

Clever. Unconventional. Resourceful.
With more than 150 local artists and designers represented, i like you is redefining "handcrafted."
Pee Wee's Playhouse meets the five-and-dime. From the wall-to-wall AstroTurf to the quirky
displays and cheeky, charming merchandise, the whole store oozes creativity. This is where Alice
buys handcrafted Minnesota-made gifts to send to her friends in Wonderland. Not to be missed.

Photos by Sky Blue Rose Photography

Sarah Sweet and
Angela Lessman

Q and A

People may be surprised to know...
We are closed annually on the first day of the
Minnesota State Fair. It's hands down our
favorite thing that the Twin Cities has to offer.

What or who inspired you to start your business?
We inspired each other to start i like you,
and are still continuing to do so.

How do you spend your free time?
Between running our business and our
families, there isn't a whole lot of free time.
But when we do find the time, we love cooking
and crafting, especially with each other.

What is your indulgence?
Flea markets, garage sales, road trips,
and sneaking off to the movies.

Happiness

Tranquility

Rejoice

Patricia Hefferan

Q and A

What are your most popular products or services?
Our unique and unusual collection of artisan jewelry, and our eco-friendly assortment of handmade, local, and fair-trade products.

People may be surprised to know...
Inizio means "beginning" in Italian. It was the beginning of a new, exciting venture for me when I started the business 10 years ago.

What or who inspired you to start your business?
I've always had a bit of entrepreneurial spirit in me. It was a goal of mine since high school to have my own business.

What do you CRAVE? In business? In life?
More time! I always want to do more in all aspects of my life. There is so much to experience and enjoy.

INIZIO

2309 W 50th St, Minneapolis, 612.886.3535
iniziogifts.com, Twitter: @Iniziogifts, facebook.com/Iniziogift

Sassy. Classy. Unexpected.
A true neighborhood gem, Inizio is a boutique filled with fun gifts, clothing, artisan
jewelry, cards, and baby gifts. One can easily find great gifts under $25 for all
occasions. Offering products that are local, handmade, and recycled as part of the
merchandise mix, Inizio provides a delightful experience for the discerning shopper.

Photos by Jessica Barker Photography

Kari Schardin

Q and A

What are your most popular products or services?
Pillows, art, lamps, and color consultations.

People may be surprised to know...
My store isn't as contemporary or as modern as some would think. We carry many pieces that could be used in any home setting.

How do you spend your free time?
Reading great mystery novels and spending time with my friends and family.

What is your indulgence?
Loads of coffee every day, a great pair of shoes, chocolate, wine, movies, family, working out, music, friends, and good food.

What do you CRAVE? In business? In life?
Total prosperity, good health, and complete happiness.

INTERIOR MOTIVE

116 Main St S, Stillwater, 651.430.1357
iminteriormotive.com

Vibrant. Stylish. Fresh.
Interior designer Kari Schardin was inspired to open a new and unique home accent store amidst the great antique stores in beautiful, historic downtown Stillwater. Interior Motive provides everything from bath scrubs and lotions, to area rugs and lighting, to accent furniture and candles. The store brings a contemporary and transitional feel to the St. Croix Valley without being too modern. Whether your home is traditional or contemporary or somewhere in between, you will always find something at Interior Motive.

Photos by LD Photography

IRELY BY SAIREYG

Twin Cities
irelyonline.com, Twitter: @irelybysaireyg

Elegant. Unique. Classy.
Irely by SaireyG offers intimates with modern, classic beauty, and everyday function. The only undergarments with a hidden pocket sitting in the small of your back, Irely gives women a secret side; a place for anything from cash and ID to small iPods and electronic devices. You can even sneak in a note for a special someone! These intimates are glamorous, comfortable, and functional.

Sairey Gernes

Q and A

What are your most popular products or services?
Our underwear! People love our lace and fabric, so no matter what style, the fit and feel is luxurious and flattering.

What or who inspired you to start your business?
The desire to design intimates that are beautiful, comfortable, and functional, so you can dress in fabulous foundations daily.

What business mistake have you made that you will not repeat?
When our manufacturer made a huge goof on our initial order, I wasn't as demanding as I should have been.

What do you CRAVE? In business? In life?
In business, developing a trusted brand of fabulous products. In life, never having to say, "I wish I would have…"

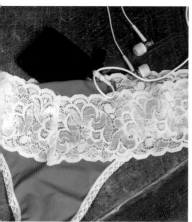

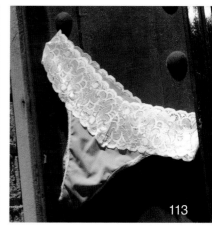

Michele Nadeau

People may be surprised to know...
Jaide is one of only a few salons in Minneapolis offering chemical-free hair color. We are big fans of Mastey color products, which are free of ammonia and other chemicals known to be harmful. With their products, I can continue to work safely throughout my pregnancy. Jaide was featured on a national CNN segment about the growth of organic hair care.

What or who inspired you to start your business?
After spending years working within the fast pace of retail salons, I wanted to create a more peaceful, creative atmosphere that promoted a balanced lifestyle. I wanted Jaide to be a place that uplifts, soothes, and provides a respite for clients, as well as a nurturing environment for stylists.

JAIDE SALON AND BOUTIQUE

4651 Nicollet Ave S, Minneapolis, 612.825.2696
jaidesalon.com, facebook.com/jaidesalon

Organic. Refreshing. Creative.

Visit Jaide Salon and Boutique once, and chances are, you'll be hooked. The sunny, art-filled space is an inviting destination for creativity and comfort. Jaide offers a full line of organic hair, skin, and make-up services and products. Committed to an all-natural approach, Jaide is a flagship salon for Simply Organic hair-care products.

Who is your role model or
mentor?

"*I am inspired by
our fantastic local
chefs and farmers
who are committed
to the local
food movement.
The Twin Cities
has a fantastic
food scene!*"

Molly Herrmann of Tastebud

JOYNOELLE

312 W 42nd St, Minneapolis, 612.209.7822
joynoelle.com, Twitter: @joynoelle, facebook.com/joynoelledesign

Stylish. Unique. Timeless.
Joynoelle is the signature line of Minneapolis-based designer, Joy Teiken. The Joynoelle
ready-to-wear, bridal, and custom collections take inspiration from classic lines, lush
fabrics, and playful details. Over the past six years, this award-winning designer
has been featured in many national and international publications, dressed several
Hollywood stars, and participated in runway and trunk shows all over the country.

Photos by Eliesa Johnson of Photogen Inc.

118

Joy Teiken

Q and A

People may be surprised to know...
I lived in Southern Africa for almost
three years with the Peace Corps, and
my Setswana name is Boitumelo.

What or who inspired you to start your business?
The Miss America Pageant. When I was a little girl,
I would draw and make paper doll pageant gowns.

What business mistake have you
made that you will not repeat?
Taking people on their word and not seeing things
in writing before trusting them with money.

What is your indulgence?
Spending time swimming, laying on the
dock, and collecting rocks at the lake.

Where is your favorite place to
go with your girlfriends?
The Grand Café for wine and yummy food.

Q and A

What are your most popular
products or services?
Our great staff specializes in helping you put
your "look" together—as long as it takes.

People may be surprised to know...
We always "tuck a good thought" into
every package that leaves our store.

What is your indulgence?
We love finding small chef-owned
restaurants in any city we visit!

What do you CRAVE? In business? In life?
Helping each customer look and
feel her best. It's our passion!

Judith McGrann and Meghan McGrann

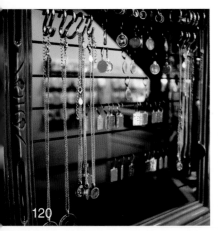

JUDITH MCGRANN & FRIENDS, INC.

4615 Excelsior Blvd, Minneapolis, 612.922.2971
judithmcgrannandfriends.com

Fresh. Fun. Friendly.

This mother-daughter boutique has been a vibrant, uplifting, and welcoming Twin Cities destination for nearly three decades. They specialize in high-quality, easy-to-wear clothing, and offer an ever-changing mix of jewelry, accessories, and one-of-a-kind finds. Customers rave about the service, the comfortable environment, and the joy of knowing they'll leave with a look that's truly their own.

JUST BLOOMED

5255 Chicago Ave S, Minneapolis, 612.600.9033
just-bloomed.com, Twitter: @justbloomed

Fresh. Chic. Stylish.
Just Bloomed is a fresh floral design studio specializing in weddings and events. Owner Jackie Just is sought after for her artistic ability to bring a client's vision to life, her signature "clutter-free" look, and elegant designs. Just Bloomed's work can be seen in local and national publications, as well as TV shows, such as ABC's *Extreme Makeover: Home Edition*.

Q and A

People may be surprised to know...
I've never received any formal floral design training. I grew up watching my grandmother design flowers and my mother make tabletops fabulous, but never went to flower "school."

What or who inspired you to start your business?
My friend Kelly once asked me, "what's the one thing you can't not do?" Mine was buy flowers (anywhere and *everywhere*)!

What business mistake have you made that you will not repeat?
I took on too many events in the beginning. Now we take on no more than two weddings or large events per weekend.

How do you spend your free time?
Checking out new restaurants, cooking, practicing photography, and walking around the Minneapolis lakes with my husband and our two young boys.

Jackie Just

JUST TRUFFLES, INC.

1363 Grand Ave, St. Paul, 651.690.0075
justtruffles.com, Twitter: @justtruffles

Chocolatey. Sensual. Decadent.
Just Truffles was founded in 1989 with the goal of making the best chocolate truffles possible. Their truffles are made with the freshest all-natural ingredients from local suppliers. No wax or preservatives, and no sugar products are added to the truffles, and a lot of love is in each one. These award-winning chocolates have been praised by celebrities around the world.

Q and A

What are your most popular products or services?
Our best-sellling truffle is Just Chocolate,
followed by the Tenor's Temptation, which
was made for Luciano Pavarotti.

Who is your role model or mentor?
I really didn't have one. I started out stumbling,
and, amazingly, became a mentor to many others.

What business mistake have you
made that you will not repeat?
Opening a store in the Minneapolis skyway
in the Baker Center. The 50,000 that
passed everyday all wore blinders.

What do you CRAVE? In business? In life?
Giving back to my community what they
give to me through my business. That is why
we support 2nd Harvest Food Shelves.

Kathleen O'Hehir-Johnson

Q and A

What are your most popular products or services?
My new collection: statement earrings, necklaces that can be worn endless ways; fine silver Fusion; and customizable Three Sisters charm bracelets.

What or who inspired you to start your business?
I've always loved creating beautiful things. When the demand for my jewelry grew, my husband bought me a book on small businesses, and JWP was born.

What business mistake have you made that you will not repeat?
Being too general and all-encompassing in my design approach. It's important to find your individual style and stay consistent with your brand.

Jennifer Walker Peterson

JWP JEWELRY DESIGNS

Twin Cities, 612.384.4672
jwpjewelry.com, Twitter: @jwpjewelry, facebook.com/jwpjewelrydesigns

Sassy. Sophisticated. Chic.
With her innovative designs that add excitement and bring outfits to life, JWP Jewelry
Designs owner Jennifer Walker Peterson has quickly captured the attention of the
Twin Cities. JWP's sassy, yet sophisticated, jewelry is hand-crafted from unique
stones and organic materials into statement-making pieces for women looking to turn
heads. From everyday jewels to elegant bridal jewelry, JWP clients treasure their
one-of-a-kind pieces and adore the compliments they receive wearing them.

Q and A

Cara Braun
Thorpe

What are your most popular products or services?
Grades K-5: Reading and mathematics intervention, and learning disability support. Grades 6-12: Study skills and organizational coaching, ACT/SAT preparation, mathematics and sciences, and ADHD coaching.

People may be surprised to know...
I founded this business 10 years ago, and we are now a staff of 25 learning coaches, serving families throughout the Twin Cities!

What or who inspired you to start your business?
The belief that every child deserves the opportunity to feel confident and successful in the school setting.

Who is your role model or mentor?
I could dedicate an entire page: educators, mothers, women who strive to be the best they can be and are not afraid to ask for help.

Photos by Stacy Dunlap

K-12 LEARNING SOLUTIONS

Twin Cities, 612.423.2724
k-12learningsolutions.com, facebook.com/k12learningsolutions

Compassionate. Talented. Professional.
K-12 Learning Solutions is a full-service educational resource for families. Owner Cara Braun Thorpe believes that a whole-child, collaborative approach most greatly benefits a student's learning needs. K-12 Learning Solutions customizes each child's learning plan based on a variety of aspects, including academic performance, work habits, and personality. They create a goal-based plan using coaching strategies to promote academic success and confidence.

Kailen Rosenberg

 Q and A

What are your most popular products or services?
The marriage "tune-up" and restoration programs, Elite Matchmaking and custom Life Makeovers.

What or who inspired you to start your business?
The desperate need within our society to understand and experience happy, healthy, and successful relationships.

Who is your role model or mentor?
My grandmother, Theodota. She was the light, the wisdom, and the angel of my life.

How do you spend your free time?
Living, loving, and seeking wisdom to honorably experience the amazing blessings of life, my family, and the gifts surrounding us.

KAI-LEN LOVE + LIFE ARCHITECTS

810 E Lake St, Wayzata, 952.544.5683
thelovearchitects.com

Knowledgeable. Passionate. Reputable.

Kai-len Love + Life Architects is a nationally-respected firm and a leading authority on loving and living well. This unique life-design firm specializes in cultivating healthy relationships for those both married and single, and is known for representing some of Hollywood's elite.

Photos by Mark Trockman Photography, except main photo by Stacy Dunlap

KARMA

867 Grand Ave, St. Paul, 651-291-1997
karmashops.com

Affordable. Modern. Bohemian.
Karma opened in 2005 as one of the first in a new breed of fashion
boutiques in the Twin Cities. A store for that special look you won't
find anywhere else, they take pride in being able to dress women of
all ages in clothing that complements with a fresh, city twist.

Photos by Erica Loeks Photography

Jada Breuer

 Q and A

What are your most popular products or services?
Melie Bianco Handbags, Tulle, Free People, Velvet, Delux Hats, locally-made jewelry, Seychelles Shoes, and Jane Tran Hair Accessories.

People may be surprised to know...
Our prices are as varied as our clientèle. We get new merchandise in every day!

What is your indulgence?
Massages and chocolate.

What do you CRAVE? In business? In life?
I want my business to constantly evolve and change with my customer and her lifestyle. I want to also enjoy my day-to-day experience with everyone I work with and play with.

Where is your favorite place to go with your girlfriends?
Los Angeles or New York City!

Kelli Kaufer

Q and A

What are your most popular
products or services?
Interior design that is stylish and classic on
all budgets that meet my client's needs.

People may be surprised to know...
I am a triathlete. I love a challenge!

What or who inspired you to
start your business?
Family. They encouraged me to follow
my passion and be the best I can be.

Who is your role model or mentor?
My mom. She's my confidante, my biggest
supporter, and, most importantly, my friend.

What is your indulgence?
A beach, sun, and an early morning
jog with my husband.

KELLI KAUFER DESIGN

1550 Amundson Lane, Stillwater, 651.341.3946
kellikaufer.com

Innovative. Stylish. Inspirational.

Kelli Kaufer's innovative, refreshing approach to design has been acknowledged by HGTV and DIY. More than 60 of her designs are featured on *Curb Appeal*, *Sweat Equity*, *BATHtastic*, and *I Hate My Kitchen*. Let Kelli create a classic, sustainable design that says *you*! Kelli's other passion is entertaining/party planning, and her stylish tablescapes and trend-setting ideas will help you host a party in style.

Photos by LD Photography

135

Amanda
Kautt

Q and A

People may be surprised to know...
Atelier means artists' workroom, so
I often show artwork in the boutique,
creating a very inspiring environment.

What or who inspired you to
start your business?
I desire a creative avenue, allowing my
artistic ability to blossom. All my passions
exist within this business: graphic design,
window displays, couture designs, working
with women, customer service, and creating a
memory and a relationship beyond one day.

Who is your role model or mentor?
My father and the family business. Look to the
horizon for your vision, and goals lie beyond.

Where is your favorite place to
go with your girlfriends?
Grabbing coffee or simply relaxing on
someone's patio with a glass of *vino*.

L'ATELIER COUTURE BRIDAL BOUTIQUE

493 Selby Ave, St. Paul, 651.602.9492
lateliercouturebridal.com, Twitter: @latelierbride, facebook.com/latelier.couture

Sophisticated. Stylish. Inspired.
L'atelier couture is the premier bridal boutique of the Midwest. Owner Amanda Kautt hand selects each gown from top-of-the-line designers in an intimate, indulgent setting. The boutique offers a very personal experience, allowing Kautt to share her passion for bridal and fashion with each and every bride.

LA COCINITA RESTAURANTE

338 5th Ave N, Minneapolis, 651.439.2795
lacocinitarestaurante.com

Charming. Cozy. Unique.
La Cocinita is a three time winner of St. Paul's Cinco de Mayo Fiesta salsa suave contest for best mild salsa. A slow food restaurant with unique dishes inspired by Mexican family recipes—ingredients are the freshest possible, sauces are made from scratch, entrees are made with love and oven-baked—for that home, hot, fresh flavor. La Cocinita serves great food and tasty Margaritas with a smile.

Angelina
Rodriguez Corbett

Q and A

What are your most popular products or services?
Marbled Enchiladas, with caramelized onions
and juicy mushrooms, Mexican cornbread bake,
and always the creative specialty of the week!

How do you spend your free time?
Menu planning, cooking at home, looking up
recipes online, reading, and gathering with
family and friends as much as possible.

What is your indulgence?
A good cosmopolitan and flat bread chorizo pizza!

Where is your favorite place to
go with your girlfriends?
Any place we can talk and catch
up on each others lives, usually a
restaurant or one of our homes.

Who is your role model or mentor?
My mom, dad, and husband for always
displaying a great work ethic and
staying positive in any situation.

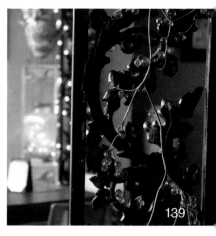

Jennifer Carpenter, Sally Clayburn, and Diane Wissink

Q and A

People may be surprised to know...
We carry a large selection of French handbags and totes from Longchamp, and fashionable Juicy Couture handbags, jewelry, and accessories.

What or who inspired you to start your business?
On a mother-daughter trip to Paris, we fell in love with the city's beautiful parfumeries, boutiques, and fabulous products.

What business mistake have you made that you will not repeat?
Buying commercial perfume lines. People want to smell quality, unique scents that they haven't seen in traditional department stores.

What is your indulgence?
Beautiful antiques, display pieces, and perfume bottles from France.

LA PETITE PARFUMERIE

287 Water St, Ste 100, Excelsior, 952.475.2212
lapetiteparfumerie.com, facebook.com/lapetiteparfumerie

Luxurious. Exclusive. Elegant.
La Petite Parfumerie, Excelsior's premier beauty and fragrance boutique,
offers anti-aging skin care from Kiehl's, Caudalie, and Fresh. Find your perfect
scent from more than 150 specialty perfumes, such as Bond no. 9, Creed, and
Acqua di Parma, with help from owners Diane, Jennifer, and Sally.

What is your indulgence?

"Champagne in the afternoon!"

Michelle Gayer of Salty Tart

LADYSLIPPER BOUTIQUE

4940 France Ave, Edina, 952.224.1900
ladyslipperboutique.com

On-trend. Stylish. Affordable.
Ladyslipper Boutique is a contemporary women's shoe and accessory boutique
located in Edina's charming 50th and France neighborhood. Think of it as your
dream closet filled with shoes, handbags, and jewelry, hand selected by three
fashion-obsessed women. Ladyslipper is recognized for trend-forward shoes and
accessories by local publications, bloggers, and fashion enthusiasts alike.

Photos by Stacy Dunlap

144

Amanda Rose, Sacha Martin, and Allison Mowery

 Q and A

People may be surprised to know...
We remember what we wore to any and
every event in the last decade!

What or who inspired you to start your business?
An unfilled niche. A shoe boutique that offers
something for everyone without designation
by price. There really is no reason that a
cute $48 sandal cannot be sold next to
a $300 pump, as long as they have one
thing in common: They are both cute!

How do you spend your free time?
Scouring fashion magazines for what is next.

Where is your favorite place to
go with your girlfriends?
Bergdorf Goodman in NYC. So many
people looking so incredibly chic. Bar
La Grassa in Minneapolis for delicious
food and great atmosphere.

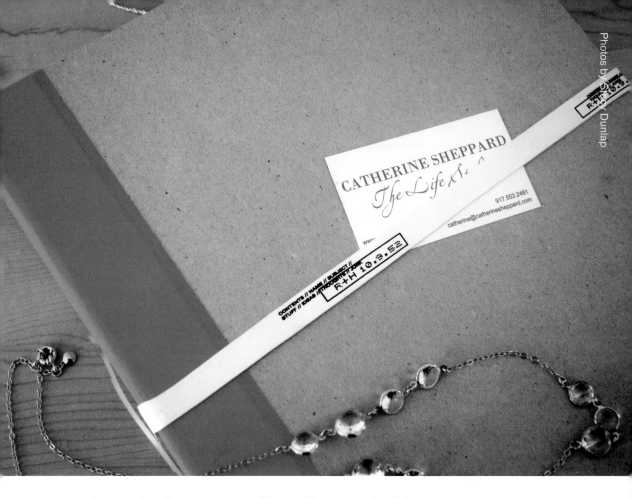

CATHERINE SHEPPARD
The Life Styled

917.553.2481

catherine@catherinesheppard.com

CONTENTS // NAME // SUBJECT //
STUFF // IDEAS //THOUGHTS // JUNK

THE LIFE STYLED

Twin Cities, 310.954.1380
thelifestyled.com, Twitter: @thelifestyled, facebook.com/thelifestyled

Stylish. Sophisticated. Smart.
The Life Styled is a modern fashion-consulting service that specializes in helping clients create their own unique style that is perfectly tailored to their personality, lifestyle, and goals. With a wide range of services, including Fashion Feng Shui, Wardrobe Detox, Bridal Style, and Personal Shopping, The Life Styled is your guide in using fashion to transform your life from the outside in.

Catherine
Sheppard

What are your most popular products or services?
Everyone wants a Fashion Feng Shui
consultation. Once you know how to dress your
essence and intentions, anything is possible!

People may be surprised to know...
Fashion is no guilty pleasure. You can
actually change your life with what
you decide to put on your body!

What is your indulgence?
True Religion jeans, red wine, fresh flowers, OPI
nail polish, *InStyle*, J. Crew cardigans, Starbucks
white mochas, and lululemon leggings.

Where is your favorite place to
go with your girlfriends?
We'll start at the W Foshay, if we're in the mood for
a luxe evening, but we always end up at Barbette
for late night pomme frites and champagne!

147

Aurélie Spirito

Q and A

What are your most popular
products or services?
Custom-designed buffet service
transforming my customer's events into
unique experiences suiting their taste
and matching the venue's décor.

People may be surprised to know...
I did not speak English when I moved
to Minnesota three years ago.

How do you spend your free time?
Learning how to live healthily; searching
for and trying new recipes; and exercising
to stay fit and to keep up with work
and my 6-month-old baby boy!

What is your indulgence?
A veal curry with coconut milk and
brown basmati rice followed by an
organic lemon-and-meringue tart.

LILA BUFFET STYLING

Twin Cities, 612.810.7716
lilabuffetstyling.com

Tasteful. Passionate. Sparkling.

Lila Buffet Styling features elegant, one-of-a-kind buffet settings, tastefully presenting gourmet food in fabulous décor for private and business events. Aurélie's creative eye for style and passion for food drove her to develop a new concept. She designs custom menus and delivers artful presentations with authentic French flair, offering countless combinations of striking colors and themes, utilizing worldwide artifacts.

Photos by Maya K. Photography

149

Q and A

What are your most popular products or services?
The assurance I bring my clients that whatever they put on, they will confidently go about their day and never worry about what they look like.

People may be surprised to know...
My clients actually spend less on clothes because every piece works.

What or who inspired you to start your business?
When I was a wardrobe consultant at Dayton's, clients told me I was part fashion guru, part coach, part therapist. They insisted I had a special gift to offer women moving up the corporate ladder.

What is your indulgence?
Peanut M&M's.

Lisa Rubin

Photos by studioTart.

LISA RUBIN WARDROBE CONSULTING, LLC.

Twin Cities, 612.747.6695
wardrobeconsulting.net

Sophisticated. Efficient. Impeccable.
Long considered a secret weapon among the most savvy businesswomen, Lisa Rubin provides exceptional service to women of all professions and incomes. For more than 25 years, Lisa's discriminating style has commanded a level of sophistication for her clientele that has no equal in the Twin Cities. With impeccable taste and confidence, Lisa offers such incredibly effective service within every woman's budget and lifestyle, her clients return season after season, year after year.

LOCAL D'LISH

208 N 1st St, Minneapolis, 612.886.3047
localdlish.com, Twitter: @LocalDLish

Local. Fresh. Sustainable.
Local D'Lish is a gourmet market located in the historic Warehouse District of downtown Minneapolis. Most products in the store are grown or made in Minnesota and the Midwest region. Local D'Lish features fresh, organic, local produce; grass-fed and pasture-raised meats; a full line of dairy, spices, chocolates, dry goods; and much more.

Ann Yin

Q and A

What are your most popular products or services?
Our produce that is harvested daily from local organic farmers, Castle Rock Dairy, and farm-fresh eggs from Sunbarn Farm.

People may be surprised to know...
Eating local is very affordable and easy to do year-round.

Who is your role model or mentor?
Sue Zelickson (local food editor and reporter). Sue founded an organization called Women Who Really Cook, and has helped many women start their food businesses here in the Twin Cities.

Where is your favorite place to go with your girlfriends?
I love to entertain in my own home. My girlfriends are amazing cooks, so we always have the best food and drinks in the comfort of my own dining room or backyard patio.

MAHA INSPIRED ACTIVEWEAR

631 Lake St E, Wayzata, 952.873.7001
mahaactivewear.com, Twitter: @mahamoments, facebook.com/mahaactivewear

Authentic. Inspiring. Connected.
Maha offers upscale activewear and leading social-networking technologies for women and men interested in active lifestyles. Maha's brands are fresh and fashion-forward. They fit all sizes and ages and perform supremely in all level of activities. Meaning "great" in Sanskrit, Maha inspires greatness through lifestyle-driven clothing, and by creating opportunities to contribute opinions and find feedback on active lifestyle events in the community.

Krista Fragola

Q and A

What are your most popular products or services?
Maha is the place to find what's next and best for your active lifestyle. Both our clothing brands and our community resources are very popular.

People may be surprised to know...
I rode the infamous dot-com boom and bust with a venture-capital-backed company in Silicon Valley. I learned what not to do when starting a business.

Who is your role model or mentor?
My friend and our Executive Buyer, Josi Wert. To me, she is the modern, successful woman. I love her style and how she's got her finger on the pulse of what's next.

What is your indulgence?
Jackets of all varieties. There's never any room in my coat closet when guests come over!

Darcy Beberg

 Q and A

What are your most popular products or services?
Our unique lamps with exquisite shades and trims, Fleur de lis and crown accessories; they are unlike any other.

What or who inspired you to start your business?
My love of shopping, decorating, and the hunt for that perfect item.

What is your indulgence?
Sleeping in late and eating pasta with lots of breadsticks!

What do you CRAVE? In business? In life?
To own 10 more stores, to save animals, shoes, greasy food, to appreciate every moment, my fiancée, and to be a mother.

MAISON GALLERIA

223 S Main St, Stillwater, 651.439.9285
maisongalleria.com, facebook.com/maisongalleria

Stylish. Eclectic. Fabulous.
Maison Galleria is an eclectic home decor store featuring lamps, artwork, clocks, mirrors, accent furniture, frames, candles, vases, florals, jewelry, handbags, scarves, seasonal items, and any other decorative accessory you can think of! From eclectic, to traditional, to the Tuscan sense of style, you are certain to discover just the perfect thing at Maison Galleria.

Photos by LD Photography

Q and A

What are your most popular products or services?
Language, Testament, Michael Stars, Twisted Heart, Ag Jeans, Ella Moss, Tolani and DaNang do amazing. We carry smaller unknown labels that are less expensive and are up and coming. We want to give customers a broader, yet unique selection.

People may be surprised to know...
I travel to New York and LA five to six times a year to scout out new trends and merchandise. We walk the streets to discover the best items to offer our customers. The majority of what we see doesn't work for our customer, but we cherry pick the perfect find!

What or who inspired you to start your business?
Watching my father and mother run this business and the pride they took in it, made me want to have something that was my own.

Erin Martin

MARTIN'S

1155 E Wayzata Blvd, Wayzata, 952.473.0238
212 Water St, Excelsior, 952.767.0788
martinswayzata.com

Fashion-forward. Fun. Friendly.
Successful since 1972 because of owner Erin Martin's ability to spot trends and deliver fresh pieces, Martin's is *the* boutique to shop! Erin's energy and savvy buying have taken Martin's to a new level of fashion-forward styles and exciting new labels. The newly remodeled Excelsior store boasts a hip vibe that welcomes women who come in searching for their favorite jeans or the latest Michael Stars tee. Customer service and affordability keeps fashionistas coming back year after year!

MAX'S

3831 Grand Way, St. Louis Park, 952.922.8364
stylebymax.com, Twitter: @stylebymax, facebook.com/stylebymax

Unique. Stylish. Artistic.
Max's is a boutique featuring artist-made fine jewelry, home decor, and specialty chocolates from around the world. Located at The Shops at Excelsior and Grand in St. Louis Park, Max's specializes in items not found elsewhere in the Twin Cities and is proud to have received both local and national retail awards.

Photos by Stacy Dunlap

Ellen Hertz

𝒬 and 𝒜

What are your most popular products or services?
Rings and sea salt caramels.

Who is your role model or mentor?
Anyone who takes a risk to follow
their dreams. And my mom.

What or who inspired you to start your business?
I didn't want to ever report to anyone
else again. I wanted to answer only
to myself and to my customers.

What do you CRAVE? In business? In life?
Authentic, honest relationships. I love the artist
trunk shows that we hold in the store, because
they strengthen our buyer/vendor relationships
and allow our customers to get to know the
personalities behind their jewelry purchases.

What is your indulgence?
Jewelry and chocolate, of course!

MAYA K. PHOTOGRAPHY

Twin Cities, 952.769.7915
photoscapturelife.com, facebook.com/mayakphotography

Genuine. Artful. Fun.
Maya K. Photography is the Twin Cities' photo studio that comes to you. Owner and photographer Katie Nees meets kids and families in their homes and on their terms for a simple, natural, stress-free approach to pictures. She'll capture what you love most about your lovable ones with distinctive photos that embrace the sweet realities of family life.

What are your most popular products or services?
Fun, relaxed, in-home children's portrait
sessions, followed by vibrant canvases
and custom-designed photobooks.

People may be surprised to know...
I was never the girl that always wanted to be
around kids—until I started photographing
them. Now there is nothing more
wonderful to me. I can't get enough!

What or who inspired you to start your business?
Two years of working answering phones in a dark
room with no windows for eight hours a day!

What business mistake have you
made that you will not repeat?
Making assumptions about people—
especially customers.

What is your indulgence?
Staying up late and sleeping even later.

Katie Nees

Caryn Mead Kelly and Mary Mead

Q and A

What are your most popular products or services?
Kate Spade Clothing and Jewelry, Longchamp bags, and Lilly Pulitzer Dresses are always a *must*!

People may be surprised to know...
Melly is for Mead and Kelly and we rarely disagree!

How do you spend your free time?
We are always working, but at the end of the day our family is the most important thing to us!

What is your indulgence?
A new Lilly dress for every Easter no matter where we are spending Easter, and a perfect cashmere sweater!

MELLY

3327 Galleria, Edina, 952.929.9252
mellyonline.com, Twitter: @mellyedina, facebook.com/mellyedina

Classic. Resort. Chic.

Melly is an adorable boutique located in the exclusive Galleria in Minneapolis. As a Lilly Pulitzer Via Store, they offer a full complement of Lilly Pulitzer clothes and accessories. In addition, they carry lines that complement Lilly Pulitzer, including Kate Spade handbags, apparel, and jewelry, Trina Turk, Shoshana, and Longchamp. Shop Melly for women's and children's clothing, purses, sunglasses, jewelry, and mongrammed items.

MONDE SALON

200 E Chestnut St, Ste 200, Stillwater, 651.439.2257

Accomplished. Enchanting. Welcoming.
Monde Salon is a welcoming, warm, creative environment filled with experienced staff that love what they do. Monde is a full-service day spa offering massage, manicures, pedicures, facials, airbrush makeup, and tanning, and a full-service hair salon. They also offer doctor-administered non-surgical cosmetic procedures.

Photos by Sky Blue Rose Photography

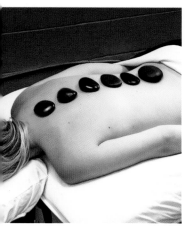

Cynthia Hagle

Q and A

What are your most popular products or services?
All hair services, massage, facials, airbrush makeup and tanning, and pedicures. Moroccanoil, TiGi, and Glo Minerals are our most popular products.

People may be surprised to know...
Our family of service providers has 10-20 years of individual experience.

Who is your role model or mentor?
My daughter is my role model. She was born knowing what is right. My sisters are my mentors. One taught me patience, and the other, endurance.

How do you spend your free time?
Relaxing with a good book or redecorating something.

MY HEALTHY BEGINNING

Twin Cities, 612.418.3801
myhealthybeginning.com, Twitter: @myhealthybeginn, facebook.com/myhealthybeginning

Natural. Wholesome. Valuable.
My Healthy Beginning is the magazine for naturally raising families, where moms find substantive content to support their desire for healthy family living. 2010 marks year five, and the first annual My Healthy Beginning Experience event, where you'll find the pages of *My Healthy Beginning* brought to life.

Nichole Hirsch Kuechle

Q and A

What are your most popular products or services?
My Healthy Beginning print magazine and our annual My Healthy Beginning Experience event.

What or who inspired you to start your business?
The desire to spend quality, focused time at home with my children, alongside the desire to create meaningful work within the community.

How do you spend your free time?
Living the content of our pages: eating well, being active in the outdoors, creating a life with my husband and children, and personal development.

What is your indulgence?
Solo retreats ... which are few and far between with young children and a young company.

Where is your favorite place to go with your girlfriends?
Someone's home for a made-from-scratch dinner, refreshments, and authentic conversation.

Kelissa Stempski and June Berkowitz

Q and A

What are your most popular products or services?
Espresso, organic oatmeal, rosemary egg salad, and customer service like no other.

Who is your role model or mentor?
My daughter, Kelissa, and the inspirational MarieRenee, who is an 100-year-old Parisian entrepreneur with attitude and style.

What is your indulgence?
Caramel rolls from St. Paul's Swede Hollow Cafe, and trips to Paris.

Where is your favorite place to go with your girlfriends?
The Trylon Theater in Minneapolis, and W.A. Frost's patio, right across from Nina's.

NINA'S COFFEE CAFÉ

165 Western Ave N (at Selby), St. Paul, 651.292.9816
facebook.com/ninascoffeecafe

Eclectic. *Dolce*. Warm.

A little New York, a little Paris, in Saint Paul's Cathedral Hill. Nina's Coffee Café is a neighborhood spot in the historical Blair Arcade Building above Garrison Keillor's bookstore. This is a great place to cozy up (PDA allowed) with a good book, a neighbor, or a business partner. It's home to local artists, writers, and musicians. Free Wi-Fi and plug-ins available. Owner June Berkowitz and her daughter, Kelissa Stempski, are looking forward to the opening of their European-inspired clothing boutique, Allee, coming in August of 2010.

Photos by Erica Loeks Photography

What business mistake have you made that you will not repeat?

" *Delivering a wedding without makeup on.*
I always forget about the groomsmen! "

Summer Harsh of Summer Harsh Botanical Artistry

Q and A

Susan Sun

What are your most popular products or services?
Alexander McQueen silk scarves, denim by J Brand, Current/Elliott, and Joe's, fun tops by Catherine Malandrino, dresses by Diane Von Furstenberg, and Alice and Olivia. Handbags from Mulberry and Valentino are a big hit as well.

What business mistake have you made that you will not repeat?
Owning a small business is all about making mistakes and learning from them. When we first opened, we ordered too much inventory, and it started to arrive two months before construction was finished!

What is your indulgence?
Handbags and shoes! I love them both because they won't ever betray you, regardless of your shape and age.

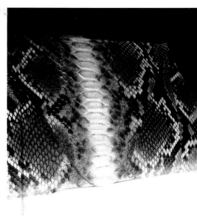

OPM BOUTIQUE

3700 Grand Way, St. Louis Park, 952.567.7399
opmboutique.com, Twitter: @opmboutique

Stylish. Posh. Contemporary.
When people first visit OPM, there is a recurring theme: "this reminds me of New York," and "I didn't know I could find these designers in the Twin Cities" are common compliments. OPM's goal was to provide a friendly, upscale boutique in a unique atmosphere that offers the designers our growing cities crave.

PAPERISTA

Twin Cities, 612.886.3470
paperistashop.com, Twitter: @paperista, facebook.com/paperista

Memorable. Fashionable. Lovely.
PAPERISTA is a custom stationery studio specializing in letterpress printing. Designs for wedding, baby, and social events bring the joy and thrill back to sending such special pieces in the mail. Inspired by fashion and known for inventive uses of color, PAPERISTA is continually recognized for memorable stationery that leaves recipients saying, "*wow*."

where life's joyous occasions
and stylish design meet on

... *paper*

Photos by Red Ribbon Studio

Q and A

What are your most popular products or services?
Wedding invitations, because of complete customization, baby shower invitations/announcements that complement nursery decor, and desk stationery that matches your personality.

People may be surprised to know...
Before PAPERISTA, I directed large annual galas in New York, San Francisco, and Los Angeles with celebrity involvement and national media exposure.

Who is your role model or mentor?
I aspire to reach the stature and brand recognition of Kate Spade. Tall order, but I love all things Kate Spade and believe she's done everything true to her style.

What do you CRAVE? In business? In life?
To always be the best that I can be, and to do it gracefully, honestly, forthright, and humbly.

Antoinette

Christine Ward

Q and A

What are your most popular products or services?
Quirky, domestic gadgetry, affordable self-indulgence, and fabulous fashion accessories.

People may be surprised to know...
Patina launched Shoppe Local to highlight local talent. Long Minnesota winters cultivate creativity.

How do you spend your free time?
With friends and family up north at our cabin.

What is your indulgence?
Traveling to New Mexico. It recharges and inspires me.

Where is your favorite place to go with your girlfriends?
Getting together with all our kids and going skating at the Centennial Lakes!

PATINA

5001 Bryant Ave S, Minneapolis, 612.821.9315
1009 Franklin W Ave, Minneapolis, 612.872.0880
2305 18th Ave NE, Minneapolis, 612.788.8933
2057 Ford Parkway, St. Paul, 651.695.9955
1581 Selby Ave, St. Paul, 651.644.5444
patinastores.com

SHOPPE LOCAL

813 W 50th St, Minneapolis

Inventive. Imaginative. Irresistible.
Patina inspires with inventive, imaginative accessories for both you and your home. Located in
five diverse metro neighborhoods, each unique store offers a personal shopping experience.
Since 1993, Patina has delivered the most current urban fashion and home accessories.
Newly opened Shoppe Local highlights area artists, designers, and manufacturers.

Photos by Stacy Dunlap

179

PETUNIA'S

421 Third St, Excelsior, 952.474.0461
petuniasonthird.com

Eclectic. Ever-changing. Unexpected.
Petunia's offers an eclectic mix of treasures for home and garden: an ever-changing mix of antiques, garden statuary, crusty, old wrought iron, carefully-selected jewelry, wonderful scented candles, quirky old pictures, and unusual plants to brighten anyone's day. Come find your treasure!

Betty Sorensen

People may be surprised to know...
Petunia's is so much more than the quirky old antiques we find. We've created a wonderful miniature fairy garden complete with a cottage, a vine-covered arbor, and adorable fairies peeking out from behind the plants. We hope to inspire our customers to create their own magical place.

What business mistake have you made that you will not repeat?
Becoming too broad and losing focus on what I do best. I used to listen to others—"you should carry this or that." My philosophy now is: Buy what I love and would love in my own home. That has worked very well for Petunia's.

What do you CRAVE? In business? In life?
I want to show my customers that mixing old with new works! You can have that old, ornate, gilded chair with a crusty side table and a lovely fern in a majolica planter! There is no "formula" to decorating; buy what you love, and it can work beautifully!

Cassidy Lexcen

Q and A

What are your most popular
products or services?
Our Kerastase line and their
customizable in-salon treatments.

People may be surprised to know...
I am at heart a true cowgirl and mechanic.

How do you spend your free time?
I love being at home with my husband
and baby girl. It means I get to make the
biggest mess possible in the kitchen,
cooking and baking whatever I fancy.

What is your indulgence?
A fantastic bottle of Italian Mascato,
an indulgent dessert, and a rich cup
of coffee. All in that order, and all in
one night, and *that* is heaven.

PHATCHELLIES

11 Tenth Ave S, Ste B, Hopkins, 952.938.5402
phatchellies.com

Chic. Vivacious. Indulgent.
Phatchellies is Minneapolis' best-kept secret. Each stylist came from some of the most high-end salons in Minneapolis, before Phatchellies even opened its doors, making them an advanced team of experts that are hard to match. Enter the salon, and be pampered by expert talent that will cater your every need.

Photos by Maya K. Photography

PHOTOGEN INC.

Twin Cities, 651.494.2257
photogen-inc.com, Twitter: @photogeninc, facebook.com/photogeninc

Bold. Elegant. Bad ass.
Photogen Inc. is a photography studio located in the heart of North East Minneapolis.
They focus on editorial, fashion, and bold wedding photography. Eliesa and her
crew have quickly become one of the most sought-after studios in the country
and have received various national awards for their photography.

184

Photos by Photogen Inc.

Eliesa Johnson

Q and A

What or who inspired you to start your business?
I wanted to live my dream, on my terms. I was the only person who was going to make that happen!

Who is your role model or mentor?
Jay Z, Lady Gaga, and my team—I am surrounded and challenged by some of the most amazing artists!

What is your indulgence?
I absolutely love vintage film cameras. I love buying and photographing with them—it's always a surprise to see what comes out!

What do you CRAVE? In business? In life?
My purpose in life is to be the blueprint—a leader photographer to help shape a new standard for our world. I will be a legend.

PICKY GIRL

949 Grand Ave, St. Paul, 651.698.4107
pickygirlmn.com, Twitter: @pickygirlmn, facebook.com/PickyGirlMNfan

Stylish. Unique. Feminine.
Picky Girl is located in the heart of St. Paul, on Grand Ave. They offer a very stylish, yet affordable, highly edited collection of a variety of clothing, accessories, and shoes. Owner Elizabeth travels both coasts to find the best selections from designers. Picky Girl has been voted Best Women's Boutique by *MN Monthly Magazine*, Best Women's Clothing by *City Pages*, and Hottest Local Boutique by *VitaMN*.

Elizabeth Varghese

What are your most popular products or services?
Our dresses are hugely popular. They are so unique and original! We carry a *true* premium denim, "Fidelity." I can hardly keep them in stock!

People may be surprised to know...
That I have been in the retail industry buying and managing for more than 12 years!

What or who inspired you to start your business?
While working for a large retail corporation in 1999, I knew that I was destined to start my own company. So I wrote my business plan and opened in 2006.

What do you CRAVE? In business? In life?
I crave equality for women! We have come so far, but there is still so much more to do. I am constantly reading and researching what is going on with women all around the world. Because of my business, I am able to support organizations that support women.

picky girl

 Q and A

Marie Suchy

What are your most popular products or services?
Gowns, gowns, and more gowns!

People may be surprised to know...
I am not a girly-girl, which you would expect for this type of business.

How do you spend your free time?
At the hockey rink! All three chidren are playing hockey.

What is your indulgence?
Champagne ... I love it!

What do you CRAVE? In business? In life?
I crave happiness not only for my family and myself, but also for every bride that walks through my boutique doors.

POSH BRIDAL COUTURE

100 W Franklin Ave, Ste 200, Minneapolis, 612.599.5759
poshmn.com, facebook.com/poshmn

Joyful. Exquisite. Divine.
Your visit to Posh Bridal Couture will be unlike any other bridal salon experience. Located on the second floor of the gorgeous Semple Mansion, Posh offers spacious appointment suites in a relaxed, intimate setting surrounded by a large selection of breathtaking gowns. You will receive undivided attention to every detail to ensure you find the dress of your dreams!

Marlys Badzin

Q and A

What are your most popular
products or services?
Emerging and hard-to-find designer shoes and
handbags, the Pumpz & Company "basics"
collection, and personal attention from staff.

Who is your role model or mentor?
I look to Bergdorf Goodman and
Barney's New York for direction.

What is your indulgence?
What else? Shoes, handbags, and jewelry!

Where is your favorite place to
go with your girlfriends?
Walking around Lake Harriet,
or going to the cabin.

What do you CRAVE? In business? In life?
I love to see women looking and feeling great
in something I know they found at Pumpz.

PUMPZ & COMPANY

3335 Galleria, Edina, 952.926.2252
pumpzco.com, Twitter: @pumpzcompany, facebook.com/PumpzCo

Classic. Sophisticated. Now.
Voted "the best" women's shoe store in the Twin Cities, Pumpz' smartly edited collections of shoes, handbags, and accessories matched with personal service makes shopping a pampered experience. Many of the designs are exclusive to Pumpz in Minnesota, including their newly launched private label shoe line.

Photos by Stacy Dunlap

191

RED RIBBON STUDIO

1526 E 46th St, Minneapolis, 952.237.9496
redribbonstudio.com, Twitter: @redribbonstudio, facebook.com/redribbonstudio

Fresh. Vibrant. Joyful.

Known for her fresh and joyful perspective, Maribeth Romslo of Red Ribbon Studio is a favorite of stylish brides for editorial visual narratives told in a vibrant documentary style. Her work has gained national attention and been featured in *Martha Stewart Weddings*, *Real Simple Weddings*, and as a "Knot Best of Weddings" photographer. Maribeth also photographs other subjects beyond weddings in her signature documentary style.

Q and A

What or who inspired you to start your business?
When I lived in New York City, I was the photo editor at The Knot. During my time in this role, I got to know the work of many talented photographers shooting weddings in an inspired way. From this experience, I was so excited to put my photographic skills to use documenting weddings, with a strong editorial influence.

People may be surprised to know...
I went to Space Camp in junior high.
I wanted to be an astronaut!

Who is your role model or mentor?
My grandmother is an inspiring model of a strong, smart, and confident woman. She was a pilot, and I always loved her flying stories and admired her spirit of elegant independence.

What do you CRAVE? In business? In life?
Joy, love, respect, passion, balance, and laughter.

Maribeth Romslo

193

RED ROVER KIDS

214 Main St S, Stillwater, 651.351.7711
redroverkids.com, Twitter: @, facebook.com/redroverkids

Fun. Immature. Classic.
Red Rover Kids is a store for kids and kids at heart. Red Rover has a great
selection of stylish and fun kids shoes, gifts, toys, books, and infant items.
Their focus is on fun, well-designed products—especially the classics.

Kristi Raney

People may be surprised to know...
We focus on young children, but
we have fun gifts for all ages.

What or who inspired you to start your business?
I've always imagined having a kids' shop, and
once my daughter was born, things fell into place.

How do you spend your free time?
What free time? I don't want free time yet. I am
planning things for future free time, though!

What is your indulgence?
Pizza and red wine. I can't stay away
from a good cheeseburger, either.

What do you CRAVE? In business? In life?
Spending as much time as possible with my
family. It is also why I have this business—I am
with them all day, every day. Kids grow so fast,
and I get to see every second *while* working!

Red Stag Supperclub

RED STAG SUPPERCLUB

509 1st Ave NE, Minneapolis, 612.767.7766
redstagsupperclub.com, Twitter: @RedStagNE, facebook.com/RedStagSupperClub

BRYANT LAKE BOWL

810 W Lake St, Minneapolis, 612.825.3737
bryantlakebowl.com, Twitter: @bryantlakebowl, facebook.com/BryantLkBowl

BARBETTE

1600 W Lake St, Minneapolis, 612.827.5710
barbette.com, Twitter: @barbetteMpls, facebook.com/BarbetteMpls

Sustainable. Zero-Waste. Fun.

Kim re-opened Bryant Lake Bowl in 1993, re-imagined Cafe Wyrd into Barbette in 2001, and built Red Stag Supperclub in 2007. Red Stag is Minnesota's first LEED-CI certified restaurant, and the nation's 17th. The restaurants focus on using as many sustainable and locally-sourced ingredients as possible, and all of the locations compost their waste.

Portrait by Jessica Barker Photography

Kim Bartmann

Q and A

What are your most popular products or services?
Good food, good parties, and entertainment.

People may be surprised to know...
We subsidize employee health insurance.

Who is your role model or mentor?
Judy Wicks, founder of White Dog Café in Philadelphia. Odessa Piper, Alice Waters, Brenda Langton, Anna Christoforides, Nan Bailly, Pam Sherman, and Lynn Alpert.

What is your indulgence?
Cheese curds and Summit, followed by a skyride to the cream puff booth ... followed up by a walk to Ye Olde Mill or a ride on the Zipper.

Where is your favorite place to go with your girlfriends?
Fish Fry!

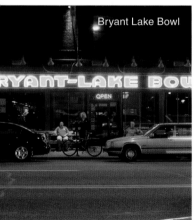

Bryant Lake Bowl

Bryant Lake Bowl

Barbette

Erin Newkirk and Renée Walter

Q and A

What are your most popular
products or services?
Modern stationery, calling/business cards,
invitations, announcements, personalized
address stamps, and greeting cards.

People may be surprised to know...
We are a small (but mighty!) company.
Most people take a look at our breadth
of product offerings and think we have
scores of employees. We don't. What
we have is a core team of incredibly
talented professionals who care deeply
about the work they do for our clients.

What do you CRAVE? In business? In life?
To make relationships stronger for our
customers and ourselves. At the heart
of meaningful correspondence is a
desire to move relationships forward.

REDSTAMP.COM

Twin Cities, 1.877.405.2270
redstamp.com, Twitter: @redstamp, facebook.com/redstamp

Stylish. Modern. Personal.
RedStamp.com is on a mission to make correspondence easy, stylish, and graceful.
The rise of social media has created more ways than ever to communicate, so their
charge is to blend the ease of e-communication with the grace of stylish correspondence
by offering practical options, personal service, and great products for every budget.
As seen in *Oprah Magazine*, *Town & Country*, *Real Simple*, and more!

Photos by Stacy Dunlap Photography

What is your indulgence?

"

*Sleeping in
late and eating
pasta with lots
of breadsticks!*

"

Darcy Beberg of Maison Galleria

RUSSELL+HAZEL

4388 France Ave S, Minneapolis, 952.279.1361
russellandhazel.com

Fresh. Humorous. Functional.
Welcome to the center of the work/style universe. In the Minneapolis store, russell+hazel's passion for stylish organization finds its ultimate expression. With new and exclusive products and "fitting desks" that let you take our systems for a spin, the store is a year-round destination for shopping, events, and ideas.

Chris Plantan

Q and A

What are your most popular products or services?
Our signature and mini binders are the hallmark of our collection and continue to be our best sellers.

People may be surprised to know...
My favorite color is white.

What or who inspired you to start your business?
My family and co-workers inspired me when we were unable to find quality school supplies and work tools.

How do you spend your free time?
Reading books and taking walks.

What is your indulgence?
An afternoon nap.

What do you CRAVE? In business? In life?
I crave manageable schedules, both professionally and in my personal life.

203

 Q and A

What are your most popular products or services?
Coconut macaroons, savory pastries, and pastry-cream-filled brioche.

People may be surprised to know...
I was nominated for a James Beard Award in 2002, as well as in 2010.

What business mistake have you made that you will not repeat?
Buying used equipment.

How do you spend your free time?
Rollin' with my ladies! Isabella and Ava, my two dream girls.

What is your indulgence?
Champagne in the afternoon, bitches!

Michelle Gayer

SALTY TART

920 E Lake St, Minneapolis, 612.874.9206
saltytart.com, Twitter: @thesaltytart, facebook.com/SaltyTart

Rustic. Sassy. Tasty.
The food philosophy at Salty Tart is "baking with integrity." That means baking fresh every morning, focusing on seasonality, and using as many local and organic products as possible. Each pastry, cookie, cupcake, boule, and baguette is made with lots of *love*. Sweet or savory, we've got what you *crave*!

SAVORIES BISTRO AND ON THE ROCKS LOUNGE

108 N Main St, Stillwater, 651.430.0702
savoriesbistro.com, facebook.com/savories.bistro

Hand-crafted. Eurocentric. Locavore.

Nearly 20 years on Main Street and a repertoire of 300+ seasonally focused dishes explains why Savories Bistro is a neighborhood favorite. "Locally grown" is a priority for owner Kristin Klemetsrud, whose hand-crafted cuisine and original recipe desserts have achieved almost cult status. When you visit Stillwater, Savories Bistro is the one place you won't want to miss.

Kristin Klemetsrud

Q and A

What are your most popular products or services?
Sustainable cuisine—we source locally. Popular recipe requests include our tomato bisque, scones, and pistachio chicken stuffed with chevre and chutney.

People may be surprised to know...
That we have started a food and wine tours to France business called Taste Beyond Paris.

What or who inspired you to start your business?
My grandmothers. One who cooked, and the other who didn't have to. One taught me the delights of cooking, the other, the finer points of hospitality; a perfect pairing.

What is your indulgence?
Coffee. Tanzanian peaberry roasted at J&S Bean Factory. When I can really start my day out right it begins with the first cup sipped in bed while I read (or watch the local news).

SERIFINA

436 2nd St, Ste 101, Excelsior, 952.474.2100
serifina.com

Unique. Classic. Bright.
Serifina is a boutique specializing in unique, classic items that can be monogrammed. They have a wide variety of interesting and beautiful gifts for children, women, and men. Serifina prides itself on making shopping fun and convenient for gift giving. They help clients choose the appropriate gift, give expert advice on monogramming styles, gift wrap, and even send the finished product.

Photos by Shelly Mosman Photography

Carol Steiger

 Q and A

What are your most popular products or services?
Our most popular products are baby blankets, cosmetic bags, totes, and stamped or engraved jewelry. We also monogram many items that customers bring in—it's all done on-site!

People may be surprised to know...
Serifina means "beautiful writing."

What or who inspired you to start your business?
Kelly Harrington started Serifina a few years ago. I was a customer in her shop and just loved everything! She wanted to go a different direction, so I took it over—I'm loving it!

What is your indulgence?
By day, I love fresh chocolate chips cookies right out of the oven with a big glass of milk. By night, a rum 'n' coke with a big bowl of popcorn!

Q and A

What are your most popular products or services?
Wedding and "post wedding" packages. On-site portrait sessions of expecting mothers, infants, children, and families. We offer a wide selection of albums and coffee table books. Also, custom cards and announcements designed with each client's unique style in mind.

People may be surprised to know...
That I started getting into photography when I was about 12. I shot with my dad's old 1950s film camera and developed each print by hand in the dark room.

What business mistake have you made that you will not repeat?
It's important to keep balance in your life. When you have a super fun job, it doesn't feel like work. Before you know it, you haven't seen your husband (let alone your friends) in days/weeks.

Jennie Sewell

SEWELL PHOTOGRAPHY

5255 Chicago Ave S, Minneapolis, 612.799.1245
sewellphotography.com, facebook.com/sewellphotography

Unobtrusive. Authentic. Captivating.
Sewell Photography specializes in a documentary style of photography, including weddings, on-site portraits of expecting mothers, infants, children, and families. Jennie Sewell's unobtrusive style allows her to capture her subjects in their most authentic state. She tries to highlight every individual's unique beauty and personality.

 Q and A

Nikol
Gianopoulos

People may be surprised to know...
I rent the sewing studio for $5 per hour!

What business mistake have you
made that you will not repeat?
I paid a lot of money to be part of a
tradeshow that, let's just say, wasn't
what I thought it would be.

What is your indulgence?
Fabric. If I like it, I'll buy it! I'll find a
use for it eventually. All you sewers
know what I'm talking about.

Where is your favorite place to
go with your girlfriends?
Twice a year, about 10-15 of us go "up
North" to a quilt camp for a week. It is the
most relaxing time of the year for me!

SEWTROPOLIS

5 W Diamond Lake Road, Minneapolis, 612.827.9550
sewtropolis.com, Twitter: @sewtropolis, facebook.com/sewtropolis

Creative. Unique. Cozy.

Sewtropolis is a DIY sewing studio and fabric store offering a large, spacious sewing studio equipped with everything the sewer may need, including the sewing machine. Beginning sewing classes are offered for children, teens, and adults. Join Sewtropolis for monthly Sit & Sews, and get inspired to finish those languishing projects!

Photos by studioTart.

Donna Kane and Cheryl Sattervall

Q and A

What are your most popular products or services?
We carry the most flattering, one-of a-kind dresses, sportswear, jewelry, and handbags. We also have the most exceptional shoe store in Wayzata.

People may be surprised to know...
Side Door Ltd. has been in business for 28 years and a mother/daughter team for 18 years!

Who is your role model or mentor?
Three role models of ours are also former partners: Ginny, June, and Rosemary.

What is your indulgence?
Handbags and belts! Mochas, dark chocolate, ice cream!

Where is your favorite place to go with your girlfriends?
Happy hour! Or for a walk!

214

SIDE DOOR LTD.

647 E Lake St, Wayzata, 952.473.1937
facebook.com/sidedoorboutique

Chic. Timeless. Fun.

Side Door Ltd. has created the atmosphere of a chic New York City boutique with edgy to classic fashions, paired with the perfect accessory, shoe, handbag, belt, `or scarf. Owners Donna Kane and Cheryl Sattervall cherry pick the collections each season so their customers can set the trends, not follow them. Exceptional, yet relaxed, customer service is something only found in a small boutique.

Brandyn Negri

What are your most popular products or services?
Aveda, Alora Ambiance, SWOBO, and lululemon.

What or who inspired you to start your business?
My gut! I feel that you either have it in you to own your own business, or you don't.

What business mistake have you made that you will not repeat?
Way too many to list. Beware of long timelines when you personally guarantee leases. They are a necessary evil when leasing, but make sure you fully understand the risks of signing on the dotted line.

What is your indulgence?
A weekend in San Francisco with Mario! Visiting all our favorite bakeries, farmers' markets, eating, doing yoga, and walking everywhere!

SIGH YOGA + BOUTIQUE

612 W 54th St, Minneapolis, 612.824.1317
sighyoga.com, Twitter: @sighyoga

Fresh. Modern. Soothing.
Sigh yoga is a modern yoga studio offering heated vinyasa, jivamukti, hot, and restorative-style yoga. Spa-like dressing rooms have showers and full amenities. A retail boutique stocks locally-made, recycled yoga clothes, yoga mats, headbands, and other accessories. Monthly memberships, packages, and drop-in rates available. Qualified, certified yoga instructors teach all classes. The relaxing atmosphere includes music, tea, and service with a smile.

Pat Scherven

What are your most popular
products or services?
Customized skin-care treatments, including
micro-dermabrasion or specialty masks for
nourishing and hydration. Phytomer and
Epicuren are our most popular retail products.

People may be surprised to know...
That we do permanent makeup,
as well as scar revision.

How do you spend your free time?
Taking classes, working out, roller blading,
cooking, and shopping for vintage stuff.

What do you CRAVE? In business? In life?
To do my best in all areas of life, to set
examples, be aware of my options,
and recognize when I need help.

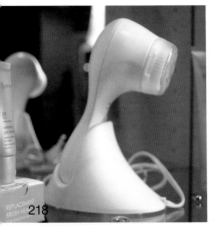

SKIN THERAPEASE

1907 E Wayzata Blvd, Ste 120, Wayzata, 952.404.0000
skintherapease.com

Peaceful. Sincere. Professional.
Skin Therapease was the first designated non-surgical clinic in the area focusing on skin health and rejuvenation. Comprehensive skin treatments encompass the whole person, inside and out, including injections for softening lines. They take great pride in their work and are honored to share more than 50 years of experience in the aesthetic industry.

SMILE NETWORK
AND THE GLOBAL COLLECTION

211 N 1st St, Minneapolis, 612.377.1800
Twitter: @smile_network

Innovative. Creative. Universally impacting.
The Global Collection is a socially conscious brand offering one-of-a-kind products and accessories for the home and individual. Every purchase funds life-altering surgeries for children born with debilitating birth defects in developing countries. All surgeries are provided by Minneapolis-based Smile Network International, a humanitarian non-profit organization.

Photos by Jessica Barker Photography

Kim Valentini

Q and A

People may be surprised to know...
Purchasing an item from The Global
Collection economically empowers artisans in
developing countries, enabling them to better
provide for their families and communities.
Additionally, your purchase helps provide a
child a second chance at life. In the process,
you acquire a unique and rare gift!

What or who inspired you to start your business?
I have always had entrepreneurial ambitions.
Approaching the age of 50 made me pause
and examine what I really wanted to be doing
for the next 50 years. My desire to pay forward
life's good fortunes and combine my passion
for travel, photography, and shopping led
to the creation of The Global Collection.

What are your most popular products or services?
Cleansing facials, progressive peels, micro-demabrasion, and brow shaping.

People may be surprised to know...
That I started this business at only 21 years old.

Who is your role model or mentor?
Sarah Kurn, an esthetician who has helped me along the way and gave me this opportunity to start my own business.

What do you CRAVE? In business? In life?
I want to be happy and confident, pass it on, and make others feel great about themselves. Beauty is within, but we can all do what we can to look and feel our best!

Stacia Wilson

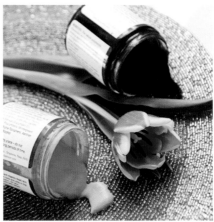

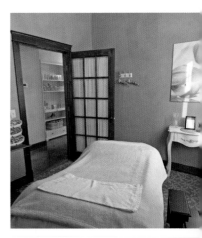

STACIA WILSON SKINCARE

86 Mahtomedi Ave, Mahtomedi, 651.426.6040
staciawilsonskincare.net

Beautiful. Girly. Healthy.

As a licensed master esthetician, Stacia has dedicated her time to learning the most advanced skin-care treatments to tackle any skin-care situation. From acne to aging, a treatment can be designed just for you. These are progressive treatments that are not just a "day at the spa." Be ready to see and feel a difference in your skin. Brow shaping and makeup are also available.

Liesl Benson and Kirsta Benson Sanchez
(co-owner Cheri Benson not pictured)

Q and A

What or who inspired you to
start your business?
Stillwater was lacking a great clothing
boutique for the modern woman, so we
decided to bring irresistible styles to town.

What business mistake have you
made that you will not repeat?
Owning a clothing boutique is a lot
of work. Learning our point of sale
software was the biggest challenge.

Where is your favorite place to
go with your girlfriends?
Marx Fusion Bistro in downtown Stillwater.
Amazing atmosphere, food, and cocktails.

What do you CRAVE? In business? In life?
Amazing fashion in business and
in life! We can't get enough!

STELLA

216 S Main St, Stillwater, 651.439.7935
stellastillwater.com, Twitter: @shopstella

Irresistible. Stylish. Sophisticated.
Stella, inspired by the modern woman, is the first high-end boutique in Stillwater.
They bring the latest fashionable trends to the Midwest and carry more than 20
unique lines. Some favorites: 213, Hazel, 1921 Denim, Joe's Jeans, William Rast,
and Michael Stars. What's to love: amazing clothing and accessories, fabulous style
advisers, and beautiful surroundings. Stella: a splurge of irresistible style!

Photos by LD Photography

Becky Sturm

Q and A

What are your most popular products or services?
Phytoceane and INtelligent Nutrients skin-care and Kinky-Curly haircare.

What or who inspired you to start your business?
My grandmother. I grew up in her beauty shop and always knew I would have one of my own.

Who is your role model or mentor?
I have always admired and been fascinated by Horst Rechelbacher, the owner and founder of INtelligent Nutrients.

How do you spend your free time?
With my family and friends, doing nothing or everything.

What do you CRAVE? In business? In life?
Family, friends, clients, and vodka with olives.

STORMSISTER SPATIQUE

635 S Smith Ave, St. Paul, 612.716.5480
stormsister.biz, Twitter: @stormsister, facebook.com/stormsistersspatique

Groovy. Cool. Brilliant.

StormSister Spatique is a kitschy beauty shop nestled neatly at the top of the Smith Avenue High Bridge in St. Paul. What began as an online business several years ago has evolved into an artsy beauty boutique. By the way, PEZ is the official store candy, so enjoy some during your shopping experience!

What do you CRAVE? In business? In life?

" *Laughter. It makes the "lows" easier and the "highs" even better.* **"**

Heather Thomas of Gigi's guide

STUDIO CATES

118.5 E Chestnut, Stillwater, 651.230.1153
studiocates.net

Friendly. Fun. Fearless.
Studio cates embraces all of our body parts. When our emotions are in distress, our health is compromised. It is important to create balance in your life by nurturing your whole body, which includes mind, body, and spirit. Enjoy studio cates with others in one of their many group classes, or on your own with a certified Pilates or fitness trainer.

Photos by Jessica Barker Photography

studio Cates
BE FIT | mind, body, spirit

Shawn Cates

Q and A

What are your most popular products or services?
Group fitness classes: yoga, Pilates, sculpt, Zumba, barre,etc. Also, one-on-one fitness and Pilates training.

People may be surprised to know...
I have four boys, ages 24, 21, 16, and 12.

Who is your role model or mentor?
Lonna Mosow! She taught me everything I know. My sister, Jennifer. She always has my back and encourages me along the way.

What is your indulgence?
Wine, chocolate, flowers, and jewelry!

Where is your favorite place to go with your girlfriends?
Polly's house in Palm Springs!

Summer Harsh

What are your most popular products or services?
About 80 percent of the designs I do are for weddings, from bridal bouquets to reception centerpieces. The options are endless!

People may be surprised to know...
I have had no formal training in floral design. Ten years of experience + passion for the art = Summer Harsh Botanical Artistry!

Who is your role model or mentor?
I know many gutsy women who direct their life and business with sass, flair, and success. I learn from each of them.

How do you spend your free time?
Always with friends, traveling, cooking, entertaining, and, in the summertime, anything water/sun related.

SUMMER HARSH
BOTANICAL ARTISTRY

Twin Cities, 612.998.6656
summerharshbotanicalartistry.com, facebook.com/summerharshbotanicalartistry

Fresh. Detailed. Avant-garde.
Botanical artistry is the art of taking Mother Nature's botanical creations and combining them with imagination and the unexpected to express a person's taste, style, and personality. Summer Harsh Botanical Artistry was created exclusively for event floral design. This encompasses wedding celebrations, corporate events, dinner parties, and any other event where a custom, one-of-a-kind piece of botanical art is needed.

Jennifer Safe

Q and A

What are your most popular
products or services?
Besides our variety of coffee drinks, customers
love our homemade cookies and buttermilk
scones. Also, our deli sandwiches are a hit
in the summer while sitting on our patio.

Who is your role model or mentor?
My mother taught me to be strong and never
give up. She was the strongest person I
ever knew. She was always positive.

What business mistake have you
made that you will not repeat?
Don't be afraid to ask for help. You can't do
everything yourself. I still try to do it all.

What is your indulgence?
Shopping for shoes and cooking
for family and friends.

THE SUPREME BEAN ESPRESSO CAFÉ

402 N Main St, Stillwater, 651.439.4314
facebook.com/supremebeancafe

Warm. Comfortable. Familial.
Start your day in Stillwater at The Supreme Bean Espresso Café. Friendly and family-owned since 1997, enjoy your favorite coffee drink, blended smoothies, pastries baked daily or a deli sandwich made to order. The cafe boasts indoor lounge seating with free wireless internet and outdoor seating on Stillwater's historic North Main Street. Situated perfectly between popular Pioneer Park and Lowell Park, grab a quick picnic lunch for the family.

Photos by LD Photography

SWEETS BAKESHOP

2042 Marshall Ave, St. Paul, 651.340.7138
sweetsbakeshop.com, Twitter: @sweetsbakeshop, facebook.com/sweetsbakeshop

Inspired. Scrumptious. Pretty.
Sweets Bakeshop offers daily cupcakes, French macarons, brownies, and blondies. They
keep things fresh and interesting by constantly updating the menu and using natural, local
ingredients whenever possible. By sourcing ingredients locally, they not only support fellow
small businesses, but also bake the freshest, truest flavor into their delicious treats.

Ly Lo and Krista Steinbach

Q and A

What are your most popular products or services?
Delicious cupcakes, French macarons,
and custom-designed sweets.

People may be surprised to know...
Krista served in Iraq, and Ly is a furniture designer.

What business mistake have you
made that you will not repeat?
Undervaluing our products and services.

Where is your favorite place to
go with your girlfriends?
Ly likes to disc golf and play poker. Krista
likes any place with a bottle of red or
sparkling wine for us to sit and visit.

What do you CRAVE? In business? In life?
Joy, creative freedom, and financial independence.

What are your most popular products or services?
Personalized party and catering services, and healthy boxed lunches for corporate events.

Who is your role model or mentor?
I am inspired by our fantastic local chefs and farmers who are committed to the local food movement. The Twin Cities has a fantastic food scene!

What business mistake have you made that you will not repeat?
Not hiring talented people to handle the specialized work needed to ensure that my business thrives. You can't do it alone!

How do you spend your free time?
Cooking (really!), reading, and enjoying the Minnesota parks with my family.

What is your indulgence?
Wine, wine, wine.

Molly Herrmann

TASTEBUD

920 E Lake St, Minneapolis, 651.470.1056
tastebudtart.com, Twitter: @tastebudtart, facebook.com/tastebudtart

Fresh. Entertaining. Playful.
Tastebud loves a party! With personal chef and catering services, owner Molly Herrmann delivers fresh, unique, and utterly delicious events. Through her cooking, writing and teaching, Molly engages eaters in her food philosophies: pleasing vegetarians *and* omnivores; using local, sustainable ingredients; and the joy of dining with friends and family. Tastebud also offers healthy boxed lunches for corporate events.

TIGER ATHLETICS

Twin Cities, 612.695.8770
tigerathletics.com, Twitter: @tigerathletics.com

Athletic. Authentic. Awe-inspiring.
TIGER ATHLETICS is a high-energy, mobile athletic company that provides unparalleled functional training programs for all ages. Co-founders Stacie and Chris Clark offer highly skilled, professional coaching within a dynamic, out-of-the-gym environment. TIGER ATHLETICS is a completely new paradigm in athletic training. It is real. It is intense. It is training for life.

Photos by Stacy Dunlap

Stacie Clark

Q and A

Who is your role model or mentor?
Strong women. There are many local, very successful, entrepreneurial-minded women who are wives and mothers as well as business owners. I admire them and look to them for knowledge, experience, and guidance.

What is your indulgence?
A movie and buttered popcorn, caramel-cashew trail mix, or having a moment at the coffee shop with the girls after an intense, calorie-burning, sweat-dripping, athletic workout. That's having it all!

What do you CRAVE? In business? In life?
Doing what I believe in, being consistent, cherishing the moments, and realizing every day is a gift because I am doing what I want to do.

Anna
Prasomphol Fieser

Q and A

What are your most popular
products or services?
Pad Thai and curry.

People may be surprised to know...
We gave our sweet and sour recipe
to St. Paul Public Schools. It is one of
their most popular menu items, and it
gets kids to eat their vegetables!

What or who inspired you to
start your business?
My mother, my Aunt Lam, and
my great-grandmother Mai.

How do you spend your free time?
Eating and exercising.

What is your indulgence?
Exotic fruit from Thailand.

TRUE THAI RESTAURANT

2627 E Franklin Ave, Minneapolis, 612.375.9942
truethairestaurant.com, Twitter: @truethai

Thai. Authentic. Friendly.
True Thai Restaurant is home to authentic cuisine from the Golden Kingdom,
and has long been the Twin Cities' favorite Thai restaurant.

Photos by Maya K. Photography

Photos by Eliesa Johnson of Photogen Inc.

URBAN JUNKET

Twin Cities, 612.746.1510
urbanjunket.com, Twitter: @urbanjunket

Functional. Stylish. Conscious.
Urban Junket bags are designed to meet the needs of busy, stylish fashionistas who need to carry and organize their belongings in a functional way. These handbags are unique, designed for organization, and made with the highest quality materials. Urban Junket is excited to introduce their newest collection, t.o.t.e. (To Observe The Earth), comprised of convertible tote bags and laptop messenger/backpacks. The t.o.t.e. line is made from eco-friendly materials, including organic cotton canvas, azo-free dyes, and RPET fabric made from recycled plastic bottles.

Q and A

What are your most popular products or services?
The t.o.t.e. collection bags, convertible totes and laptop messenger bags.

People may be surprised to know...
That I created a local event called Maiden Minnesota with my publicist to help bring visibility to all of the great women-owned businesses in the Twin Cities.

What or who inspired you to start your business?
My parents always taught me to believe that I could do anything I wanted if I was willing to do the work. The fact that they have always believed in me and supported me made it easier to make the leap from corporate America.

How do you spend your free time?
Running with my dog, volunteering with Free Arts Minnesota, shopping for fun trends, and seeking out sushi with friends.

Tracy Dyer

Kerry Ciardelli

Q and A

What are your most popular
products or services?
Interior design and in-home editing. Vintage
European furniture, Venetian mirrors,
luxurious candles, English silver, unique
jewelry, and several lines of bedding.

What or who inspired you to
start your business?
VICTORY was inspired by my passion
for travel, love of beauty, style,
entertaining, interior design, elegance,
and all things vintage and modern.

How do you spend your free time?
I love spending time with my daughter,
cooking, walking our dogs around Lake
of the Isles, immersing myself in design
books, and, of course, traveling to
discover unique goods for VICTORY.

VICTORY

3504 W 44th St, Minneapolis, 612.926.8200
shopvictory.com, facebook.com/shopvictory

Elegant. Chic. On-trend.
VICTORY is an enchanting Linden Hills store opened in 2003 by Kerry Ciardelli, a self-taught interior designer and entrepreneur. On her travels around the world, Kerry hand-picks an eclectic, but elegant mix of uncommon, vintage, and new items. The silver stamp of VICTORY on a beautiful black box, tied with striped grosgrain ribbon, is a sign of impeccable taste.

Photos by Stacy Dunlap

247

WRITE AWAY

Twin Cities, 612.822.0002
writeaway.com, Twitter: @writeawaypaper

Personalized. Special. Pretty.

Write Away produces uniquely personalized stationery and gifts with character and style.
The exclusive graphic collection ranges from whimsical to classic design, allowing customers
to express their own personal flair on each product. In addition to selling online, a team of
enthusiastic representatives sell Write Away products at home parties across the country.

Photos by Maya K. Photography

248

Meredith Johnson
and Sarah Graff

$\mathcal{Q}$ and $\mathcal{A}$

What are your most popular products or services?
Our calling cards that take a person from tacky
to sophisticated—no more ripping out check
deposit slips to give out personal information!

People may be surprised to know...
We live four houses from each other, and our
children are almost the exact same ages—big
reasons that our partnership works so well.

What or who inspired you to start your business?
Our desire to contribute to our families
in a creative way without compromising
our values and priorities.

Where is your favorite place to
go with your girlfriends?
Nails Only, our local salon that allows
us to bring in cocktails and treats!

Q and A

Patti Soskin

What are your most popular products or services?
Patticakes (a super-moist three-layer chocolate cake with buttercream frosting) and chicken clubs (multi-grain toast with grilled chicken, avocado, bacon, lettuce, tomato, and aioli).

Who is your role model or mentor?
My mom made incredible meals, encouraged me to make a mess in the kitchen, and taught me that food is connected to the soul.

Where is your favorite place to go with your girlfriends?
Four friends on two tubes pulled behind a boat on a lake in the sun.

What do you CRAVE? In business? In life?
In business, I crave that Yum! is a day brightener. In life, I crave bright days.

YUM! KITCHEN AND BAKERY

4000 Minnetonka Blvd, St. Louis Park, 952.922.4000
yumkitchen.com

Fresh. Friendly. Yummy.

Yum! Kitchen and Bakery is the ultimate neighborhood restaurant serving fresh and friendly food that makes you smile. The bakery offers award-winning cakes, "Seuss-like" cupcakes, oversized cookies, ever-changing morning pastries and fair-trade coffee. The kitchen prepares seasonal soups, sandwiches, salads, and entrees, alongside favorites, including chicken soup, gumbo, fancy-schmancy tuna, and tarragon chicken salads.

Intelligentsia Directory

Business-to-business entreprenesses, including coaching, marketing and public relations, photography, business consulting, and design services.

BESK & VANORSDALE
EDINA REALTY

14430 60th St N, Stillwater, 651.430.7524
msprealtors.com

Honorable. Responsible. Smart.

Besk & VanOrsdale are the first choice for sellers, buyers and investors. Backed by the strength of Edina Realty, they specialize in the St. Croix River Valley. Licensed in both Minnesota and Wisconsin, clients put their trust in Besk and VanOrsdale to help guide them through a constantly changing real estate market.

Q and A

Linda Besk and Lynn VanOrsdale

What or who inspired you to start your business?
Linda was a single mother with an empty refrigerator … Linda inspired Lynn to make a career move to real estate.

Who is your role model or mentor?
Emma Rovik, the founder of Edina Realty.

What business mistake have you made that you will not repeat?
Taking on the sale of a home when the sellers had zero motivation to sell.

Where is your favorite place to go with your girlfriends?
We love to have girls' getaways. Canyon Ranch Spa in Tucson was the most recent.

CLOTHIER DESIGN SOURCE

Twin Cities, 651.400.0652
clothierdesignsource.com

Helpful. Knowledgeable. Trend-savvy.
Clothier Design Source offers professional apparel product-development services to businesses and individuals. What does that mean, you say? They'll take your clothing concepts and make them a reality through design, technical design, sampling, sourcing, and manufacturing. Contact Clothier by phone or online for a free consultation.

Mindy Martell

Q and A

What are your most popular products or services?
Manufacturing garments is most popular. We manufacture here in Minnesota and all over the globe. No matter the order quantity, we can make it happen!

What business mistake have you made that you will not repeat?
Business partnerships are difficult. It's like a marriage, and I already have the marriage partner covered. I do not think I will ever try a partnership again but stick to joint ventures—with my husband!

What is your indulgence?
Yoga, massage, and wine.

Where is your favorite place to go with your girlfriends?
Boundary water canoe area.

ERICA LOEKS PHOTOGRAPHY

Twin Cities, 612.743.2974
ericaloeks.com, Twitter: @ericaloeks, facebook.com/ericaloeksphotography

Romantic. Artistic. Stylish.
Erica Loeks documents weddings and children, as well as editorial and portrait photography. Her work has been featured in *Minnesota Bride*, *Chicago Bride*, *Clover & Bee*, and other national publications. She shares her point of view with her clients: *document love!*

Erica Loeks

Photo by Erica Loeks Photography

Q and A

What are your most popular products or services?
Wedding and children photography.

People may be surprised to know...
I donate a portion of money from every shoot to Operation Smile.

What or who inspired you to start your business?
A friend's wedding inspired me.

Who is your role model or mentor?
Elizabeth Messina.

What business mistake have you made that you will not repeat?
Not giving myself a day off each week to relax.

How do you spend your free time?
Yoga, friends, and family.

FLOURISH

Twin Cities, 612.237.6755
flourishdesignoffice.com, flourishdesignoffice.blogspot.com, flourishdesignoffice.etsy.com, Twitter: @meg0ls0n

Smart. Fresh. Unique.
To flourish: to grow luxuriantly, to thrive. Flourish is a graphic design office that specializes in growing businesses through branding, whether it's print design, web design, or other creative marketing ideas. Flourish will work with you to identify your brand and goals, and guide you to a smart solution that will make your business thrive. A great business always starts with strong branding.

Megan Olson

People may be surprised to know...
I always begin the creative process the old-fashioned way—with a pencil and paper.

What or who inspired you to start your business?
Myself! I've always known I would love creating my own adventures in the design world. I was right.

What is your indulgence?
Books, magazines, and design blogs. Pretty much any good eye candy I can get my hands on.

Where is your favorite place to go with your girlfriends?
My house for a crafternoon with good food, good conversation, and good crafts.

GIRL.MEETS.GEEK

Twin Cities, 612.501.8159, thegirl@girlmeetsgeek.com
girlmeetsgeek.com, Twitter: @girlmeetsgeek, facebook.com/FanTheGeek

Passionate. Business-savvy. Educational.

There's only a two-letter difference between "passion" and "passing it on." Kate-Madonna Hindes is a nationally recognized, sought-after public speaker and published writer about fueling life with passionate and reachable goals using social media. Whether she's training businesses, career-coaching, or speaking about the *human* behind the media, she empowers you to make a difference in today's business.

Kate-Madonna Hindes

Q and A

What are your most popular products or services?
I offer a "dinner and a resume" package, which helps clients take time to refocus, eat, and finish their resume. It's affordable, and most importantly, fun!

What or who inspired you to start your business?
After seeing people flock to social media, but not understand the true value, I knew I had the perfect opening.

What business mistake have you made that you will not repeat?
Mistakes? There is no such thing as a mistake. There is learning, and my life has been *full* of that.

JWDA

7416 Washington Ave S, Eden Prairie, 612.597.8383
jwda.com, facebook.com/JWDAMPLS

Honest. Casual. Real.

"Concept to Completion." That is JWDA's motto. They can create, produce, and deliver your job under one roof. Their awesome lodge-style office in Eden Prairie and their golden lab, Leo, will surely greet you at the door and welcome you! Owner Sara Witta would love the opportunity to serve you in any of your creative needs.

Sara Witta

Q and A

What are your most popular products or services?
Logo design, web design, and printing services.

People may be surprised to know...
We do it all. If you need it for your company, we can supply it.

What business mistake have you made that you will not repeat?
Having a partner. It is best to do it on your own!

Where is your favorite place to go with your girlfriends?
Hunt and Gather on 50th and Xerxes.

What do you CRAVE? In business? In life?
In business, doing the best job I can, and having satisfied customers. In life, slowing down. It is going way too fast!

KATHY HANSON

Twin Cities, 952.451.0658
Twitter: @KathyHansonBiz

"Can I bottle your energy?" "I never would have thought of that!" "You get things done! I can tell you are fiercely intelligent without any fluff." Kathy Hanson's clients consider her their secret "board of directors", strategist, not-so-silent partner, and business consultant. Accomplished, with years of experience working with start-ups and Fortune 100 companies, Kathy brings fresh perspective and new passion to issues big and small. Call Kathy to learn why so many clients count on her to come up with solutions that work.

Photo by Stacy Dunlap

Kathy Hanson

Q and A

What are your most popular products or services?
Clients are so busy running a business, they often can't see straight. But I can—I help my stretched-too-thin clients get excited about solving any issue they struggle with in their business, big or small.

People may be surprised to know...
My mind operates as if I drink Red Bull all day, but I swear, I don't!

What or who inspired you to start your business?
When I was a VP of sales and marketing for a printing company, (with a brand-new MBA), I suggested offhand a cost-savings idea to a Hewlett Packard executive, and my business was born!

KIMBERLY T. WALKER
LAW OFFICE, P.A.

3300 Edinborough Way, Ste 400, Edina, 952.956.0300
kwalkerlawoffice.com

Experienced. Compassionate. Proven.

Help your family build a better tomorrow. Whether faced with divorce, child custody, spousal support, child support, or another family law matter, Kimberly T. Walker Law Office provides clients with the personal service and attention they deserve. Working with you to achieve optimal results as efficiently and cost-effectively as possible, Kimberly knows clients and their families come first.

Q and A

Kimberly Tourdot Walker

What are your most popular products or services?
Divorce, child custody, and child-support proceedings.

People may be surprised to know...
I was adopted as a baby.

What or who inspired you to start your business?
Colleagues that were thriving as solo practioners and enjoying the freedom that creating your own schedule allows.

What is your indulgence?
Bismarck donuts!

What do you CRAVE? In business? In life?
The challenge of the law and the joy that my children bring me each day.

LOVEe CONSULTS

Twin Cities, 651.494.2257
photogen-inc.com/blog/lovee-consults.html, Twitter: @photogeninc, facebook.com/photogeninc

Inspiring. Kick-ass. Remarkable.

LOVEe Consults are intensive, one-on-one, eight-hour consultations for photographers to critique their entire business. Owner Eliesa Johnson's goal is to leave her clients with a clear vision of where their business is going and give them the tools to continually be inspired. Topics covered include The Artist, Intense Critique, Goal Setting, Marketing, Submissions, Equipment and Shooting Techniques, Inspiration, and Open Q&A.

Eliesa Johnson

Q and A

People may be surprised to know...
Owning your own business is way more fun, less stressful, and easier than it may seem. We will get you there!

What or who inspired you to start your business?
I always knew I wanted to be a photographer, and, over the years, I have also developed a passion for business and inspiring others to succeed!

What is your indulgence?
Chai tea, yoga, Perez Hilton's blog, and shopping at Anthropologie!

Where is your favorite place to go with your girlfriends?
My current favorite place is Bar La Grassa—or anywhere that has a bottle of *vino* and a fabulous atmosphere!

STACY DUNLAP

Twin Cities, 612.840.0290
stacydunlap.com, Twitter: @stacydunlap, facebook.com/stacydunlap

Authentic. Eclectic. Invested.
Photographer Stacy Dunlap causally draws out the picturesque simplicities of human nature. Whether photographing people, lifestyle, or the elements, her approach is laid-back and natural. Stacy's unassuming and spontaneous personality provides her clients with a fun, relaxed, and memorable experience. You'll quickly discover when working with Stacy, nothing is ever posed—it's captured.

Photo by Stacy Dunlap

Stacy Dunlap

Q and A

What are your most popular products or services?
Lifestyle and portrait photography. Capturing people in their element.

People may be surprised to know...
I hate having my picture taken. Ironic, I know.

Who is your role model or mentor?
My grandmothers. Both were very different from one another. Luella was gentle and an observer. Alice was an artist and unpredictable.

What is your indulgence?
Vases of fresh-cut flowers everywhere, and a glass of my favorite *vino*.

What or who inspired you to start your business?
Words that photographer Jeff Lipsky shared with me: "It's about timing, tenacity, and talent, and in that order."

VIMLAB PROMOTIONS

Twin Cities, 612.229.8522
vimlab.com, Twitter: @vimlab, facebook.com/VimLabPromotions

Vivacious. Lavish. Inspiring.

VimLab Promotions is a high-energy public relations, marketing, and events firm specializing in nightlife, music, food, fashion, hotels, spas, architecture, sports, benefits, and luxury lifestyle. Established in 2003, VimLab has created original, branded events such as VimLab Boat Parties out of Boom Island and The VimLab Guac Off. High-profile lifestyle clients and small businesses are publicized both nationally and throughout the Twin Cities.

Natalie Auger

Q and A

People may be surprised to know...
I grew up in Orange County, California, and spent most of my 20s in San Francisco but feel very much at home in the Twin Cities. I really love living here, except for the winters, when I head back to California for a few weeks.

Who is your role model or mentor?
Cynthia Bowman, who gave me my first PR job in San Francisco. She has many hilarious stories of the '60s and '70s.

Where is your favorite place to go with your girlfriends?
The lounge at Bradstreet Crafthouse at Graves 601.

What do you CRAVE? In business? In life?
New experiences—I love to travel, meet interesting people from all walks of life, and discover things I didn't know the day before.

WINDMILLER DESIGN GROUP

Twin Cities, 612.616.1886
windmillerdesigngroup.com, Twitter: @windmillerdg, facebook.com/windmillerdesigngroup

Enthusiastic. Passionate. Creative.

Windmiller Design Group is a graphic design and marketing company located in the Twin Cities. Offering the essential marketing and design services that businesses need to succeed, WDG provides consistency and quality throughout the business and the brand—from logo design to print collateral, web design, and more.

Mollie Windmiller

People may be surprised to know...
Windmiller Design Group helped launch *Artful Living Magazine*, a luxury magazine of the Twin Cities.The layout is created by WDG for each quarterly issue.

What or who inspired you to start your business?
My passion for design ... *good* design. And the chance to help people that have a vision for their business to become a reality.

Who is your role model or mentor?
My parents. My dad has always been an entrepreneur, and I have learned a lot from him. My mom is a former art teacher and is now a docent at the MIA. She is a true creative. It shines through every day.

Contributors

At CRAVE Minneapolis/St. Paul, we believe in acknowledging, celebrating, and passionately supporting locally-owned businesses and entrepreneurs. We are extremely grateful to all contributors for this publication.

Amanda Buzard
graphic designer and project manager
amandabuzard.com

Amanda is a Seattle–based designer inspired by clean patterns and bold textiles. She chases many creative and active pursuits in her spare time. Passions include Northwest travel, photography, dining out, and creating community.

Nicole Shema
project manager
nicoles@craveparty.com

Nicole graduated from the University of Oregon in June 2009 with bachelor's degrees in economics and political science, and then moved back to her hometown of Seattle. She has been with CRAVE since September 2009.

Lilla Kovacs
operations manager
lilla@thecravecompany.com

Lilla has been with CRAVE since 2005. As the operations manager, she ensures that everything runs like clockwork. She loves shoe shopping, traveling, art, and her MacBook.

Alison Turner
graphic designer
alisonjturner.com

Alison is a graphic designer, seamstress, and outdoor enthusiast from Seattle. She is a supporter of the ongoing push for human rights, as well as the local food movement.

Alison Peacock
copy editor
peacockweddings.com

Alison Peacock is a writer, editor, and photographer with 18 years of journalism experience. When she's not copyediting books about savvy businesswomen, she focuses her camera on her favorite subject: weddings.

Mimi Jamaleldin
CRAVE fashion maven
mimijamaleldin@gmail.com

Girl-about-town Mimi Jamaleldin is accomplished in spotting trends and she knows what twenty-somethings want and wear at any given moment in their busy lives. She is happy to blog about it so we all know the latest!

Contributors (continued)

Clare Saunders
social media guru
Twitter: @clarefsaunders,
clarefsaunders@gmail.com

Energy abounds in Clare Saunders! Handheld device always at the ready, Clare brings insight, energy, and new ideas to clients big and small.

Stacy Dunlap
photographer
612.840.0290, stacydunlap.com

Stacy Dunlap captures the simplicities of human nature and finds the hidden beauty in things forgotten. Whether photographing people, lifestyle, or the elements, Stacy's approach is laid-back and naturalistic.

Jennifer Sellers
*photography manager,
and blog editor*
jennifersellers.blogspot.com,
jennisellers@gmail.com

Jennifer has an impressive eye for design, and an ability to keep projects organized, prompt, and profitable, as well as an exceptional gift as a writer.

Erica Loeks
photographer
612.743.2974, ericaloeks.com

Erica Loeks Photography specializes in *documenting love!* Her assignments range from portraits to lifestyle and documentary wedding work. Her photographs have been published in numerous national magazines, newspapers, and online blogs.

Jessica Barker Photography
photographer
612.267.2122,
jessicabarkerphotography.com

Jessica is a lifestyle photographer with an eye for capturing life as it is meant to be lived—freely, and without interruption. She specializes in portraits for newborns, children, families, and seniors, as well as boudoir, intimate weddings, and other events.

LD Photography
photographer
651.303.5383, lauriedick.com

Laurie Dick infuses her lifestyle and commercial photography with small-town charm, friendliness, and modern creativity. Her passion is to capture the uniqueness of individuals and natural moments to create timeless images.

Contributors (continued)

Maya K. Photography
photographer
photoscapturelife.com,
952.769.7915

Katie Nees is a people photographer. Her clients love her for capturing real-life moments from every stage of their family life, with images that are beautiful, artful, and fun.

studioTart.
photographer
studiotart.com, 651.329.7414

StudioTart. specializes in portrait, architectural, and landscape photography throughout the Twin Cities. Owner Megan Dobratz captures the colorful details of life … with a sweet little bite.

Sewell Photography
photographer
612.799.1245, sewellphotography.com

Jennie Sewell specializes in documentary-style photography including weddings, on-site portraits of expecting mothers, infants, children, and families. Her unobtrusive style allows her to capture her subjects in their most authentic state.

Sky Blue Rose Photography
photographer
skybluerosephotography.com

Linda Capra is a portrait, lifestyle, and event photographer. Her compassionate heart and perception show through her work—capturing the moments that show the essence of being, not just the subject.

Additional photography by Photomoss, Eliesa Johnson of Photogen, Inc., and Red Ribbon Studio.

Manifest by category

Manifest by category (continued)

Manifest by category (continued)

Manifest Intelligentsia Directory by category

Manifest by neighborhood

Manifest by neighborhood (continued)

Manifest by neighborhood (continued)

the CRAVEcompany™

Innovative Connections

The CRAVEcompany innovatively connects small business owners with the customers they crave. We bring together small business communities and fuel them with entrepreneurial know-how and fresh ideas—from business consulting to shopping fairs to new media. The CRAVEcompany knows what it takes to thrive in the modern marketplace. thecravecompany.com

CRAVEparty®
What do You Crave?

CRAVEparty is an exclusive, festive, glam-gal gathering of fun, entertainment, personal pampering, specialty shopping, sippin' and noshin', and just hanging with the girls.

CRAVEguides™
Style and Substance.
Delivered.

CRAVEguides is the go-to resource for urban-minded women. We celebrate stylish entrepreneurs by showcasing the gutsiest, most creative and interesting proprietors from cities all over the world.

CRAVEbusiness™
A Fresh Approach to Modern Business

CRAVEbusiness is a social, resource network for stylish innovators who own their own business, or dream of starting one. Through one-on-one consulting, workshops and red-carpet access to sage and savvy experts, entrepreneurs meet with others in their fields to get a fresh approach to their business.

Craving Savings

Get the savings you crave with the following participating entreprenesses—one time only!

5 percent off
- ☐ Galleri M.

10 percent off
- ☐ Art of Optiks
- ☐ Bibelot
- ☐ Blissful Bath
- ☐ Cocoa & Fig
- ☐ Cooqi Gluten-Free Delights
- ☐ Dichotomy
- ☐ Ditto & Co. (online with code CRAVE)
- ☐ Extrados
- ☐ Fleurish
- ☐ Flourish (online with code CRAVE)
- ☐ Garden of Eden Inc.
- ☐ Girl.meets.geek (online with code CRAVE)
- ☐ Golden Fig Fine Foods
- ☐ Inizio
- ☐ JWDA
- ☐ K-12 Learning Solutions
- ☐ Kai-len Love + Life Architects
- ☐ L'atelier couture bridal boutique
- ☐ Lila Buffet Styling (online with code CRAVE)
- ☐ Maya K. Photography (online with code CRAVE)
- ☐ PAPERISTA
- ☐ Patina
- ☐ Picky Girl
- ☐ Pumpz & Company
- ☐ Sewtropolis
- ☐ Shoppe Local

10 percent off (continued)
- ☐ Smile Network and The Global Collection
- ☐ Stacy Dunlap (online with code CRAVE)
- ☐ VICTORY

15 percent off
- ☐ Amy Zaroff Events and Design
- ☐ Camrose Hill Flowers
- ☐ Clothier Design Source (online with code CRAVE)
- ☐ Farmer's Hat Productions (online with code CRAVE)
- ☐ Flirt Boutique
- ☐ Fringe
- ☐ Martin's
- ☐ Windmiller Design Group (online with code CRAVE)

20 percent off
- ☐ Alfresco Casual Living
- ☐ Bananas for kids
- ☐ Blooma
- ☐ The Bungalow
- ☐ Café Twenty Eight
- ☐ Covered
- ☐ Darn Knit Anyway
- ☐ EuroNest
- ☐ Fusion LifeSpa
- ☐ Hunt & gather
- ☐ Jaide Salon and Boutique
- ☐ JWP Jewelry Designs (online with code CRAVE)
- ☐ Karma

Craving Savings